Poetry

Reading it
Writing it
Publishing it

Compiled and Edited by
Jessie Lendennie

salmonpoetry

Published in 2009 by
Salmon Poetry
Cliffs of Moher, County Clare, Ireland
Website: www.salmonpoetry.com
Email: info@salmonpoetry.com

ISBN 978-0-9561287-5-1

Cover photography: Book of Poetry by Olgalis, from Dreamstime.com
Typesetting & Design: Siobhán Hutson

I am deeply grateful to the poets who have contributed their expertise and time to this volume. Despite the fact that they have their own creative work to attend to, they spend hours nurturing others through teaching, workshops, festivals, and giving time-consuming advice. To James Harrold, the only non-poet in the group, I say, "I remember you in the Galway Writing Workshop circa 1984. You should have kept it up!"

JESSIE LENDENNIE

Contents

PUBLISHING IT

"I've had a classic anxiety dream recently: I'm to give a poetry reading, have my book in a pocket (how it fits in a pocket, I'm not sure, but in the dream I'm confident), am introduced, walk up to the podium, reach into my pocket, pull out my book, and it's my chequebook. At this point I wake up. It's funny, now..."

POET & SMALL PRESS PUBLISHER

Jessie Lendennie

(County Clare, Ireland)

Introduction

Type 'Poetry' into Google and you get 128,000,000 entries. *128,000,000!*

Try 'Poetry Blogs': 13,300,000. 'Poetry journals': 30,700,00. These are dizzying numbers (and growing exponentially).

These websites encompass the mad, the mundane and the marvelous. It's an awful lot of stuff about poetry. I point this out as a way to emphasise that, despite the fact that most people will go numb if you talk to them about poetry, many of them, at some time in their lives, write it, or want to write it. For a poetry book publisher, this is, potentially, a great big market. Imagine if everyone who accessed one of these websites decided to buy a poetry book! Wow, South Sea Islands here I come! Well, no, alas, it doesn't really work that way. I've used the "look at all the Internet hits for Poetry" as an argument for more funds from the Arts Council. To show that there really are people who want to read poetry books, so the Arts Council should give us more money to reach those big spenders. Hasn't worked yet.

Well, back to the real world: As an early exponent of the Internet, I've been encouraging aspiring poets to use this resource for years in the belief that the more they know the broader their choices – and minds. Perhaps many did benefit, but it's possible that many were overwhelmed with the utter vastness of it all. Given the tentative approach of most aspiring poets, it's easy to see that one could come away from an Internet search in total confusion. As with most things, information varies in its usefulness; so after considering the best way to advise aspiring poets, I've come full circle – back to the good old "here's a book, and there's a lot of good, sound advice within; based on years of experience – from reading poetry, writing poetry to selecting it for publication. Read it."

There are only a few basic things to consider when thinking about getting your poetry published. These points are made over and over again by people working in this field. Why the repetition? Is no one listening? Why don't poets follow a tried and true formula for writing and publishing? Resistance to conformity seems to be a part of the poet's psyche (or at least the poet's image). We seem to be compelled to rediscover the process for ourselves. The first stirrings of a poem is a deeply personal experience involving an intense recognition of one's own uniqueness. The feeling of discovery, which is so exciting, even addictive, is as far removed from the rough and tumble of the "marketplace" as it's possible to be. In order to protect that special part of oneself, the 'poetry' of oneself, it can be easy to fall into a kind of Protectionism of the Soul. Unwilling to move away from that special impulse, we are likely to act on intuition rather than hard logic when it comes to getting our poems out in the world. Yes, of course, poetry is not, in itself, about "how-to". It's a complex pattern made up of our own perceptions, insights, intelligence, confidence, motivation, and even self-image.

Poetry, once the province of a few, overwhelmingly male, writers, with pipes and tweed jackets (and, we mustn't forget, the whiskey bottle) now has a variety of faces, a plethora of practitioners, and, consequently, a confusion of definitions. This appears to be frightening to those who hold a single view of what poetry is, ie. "This (insert your own cultural assumption) IS what poetry should be; how it should be written; how it should be understood". On a personal note; since its beginning, Salmon has been up against a particularly narrow definition of the IRISH poem. I think of Emily Dickinson (as it happens, the poet most often quoted in these essays). We all know that she only published a handful of poems in her lifetime; but it's most fascinating to note that those poems were heavily edited to fit in with the conventional poetry of the day. How awful; hard to think of what Dickinson must have felt – like an outsider? A mere woman versifier? Glad to be part of the establishment? How is it that we embrace her poetry now, when we wouldn't have done so in her day unless it was edited to fit with the received definition of poetry? Silly question? Maybe, but it goes to the heart of how canons are established, and notions of the real meaning of poetry.

The purpose of this book is to make aspiring, and otherwise, poets aware of all the aspects of poetry, from the enjoyment of reading, to the sweat and tears of running a small press. It's crucial for a poet who is serious about her/his art to be informed. If there's one thing to keep in mind, it's that simple fact.

My specialty is, of course, the publishing of poetry. As well, over the years, I've run writing workshops, with participants ranging in age from 7 to 80. As well as keeping my publisher's eye out for poets to grace Salmon's list, I've spent a huge amount of time helping people who want to write. The Salmon website contains questions & answers about poetry and publishing – www.salmonpoetry.com. Since these points are very much part of what this book is about, I'm including the main points.

The one thing, above all, that I would advise poets to consider before approaching a publisher – even by email – is to know as much as possible about the press they are querying.

Editors look at the professionalism of each submission – not only a high standard of writing, but a clear, informative letter. It's easy to see who has put thought into their query and who hasn't. Email makes it very easy to dash off a note in a mood of "what the heck, I'll just ask", but 95% of the time such a query will either be ignored or receive a curt reply.

Take your time! Investigate! Think about why you want to publish! Do you consider yourself a professional? Are you willing to persist with your writing no matter what happens? Can you stand back and attempt an unbiased look at your work?

The following are the most common queries and requests:

1. *Please publish this poem on your website*

The poems we have on the site are all from collections we've published. The main aim of the site is to promote and sell our books. Personally, I also want to give advice; guidance through the morass that is poetry publishing today, but I can't deal with all needs and I have an obligation to the poets we publish.

2. *I don't like sending work to magazines and competitions, but I know my work is good enough to be published as a book.*

This one is complicated.

Some people despise what they see as the pretentious, insincere literary world. It certainly is desirable to have a critical sense, but not to confuse the context with the content. In other words, while any arts discipline (indeed, almost anything!) can seem corrupt from outside, unless one examines and participates in the give and take of it all (importantly adding your own experience) you are writing in a vacuum. Creativity feeds on experience – it's important to discriminate but not to block experience. It is useful to remember that what we despise and reject will haunt us; hampering creative development.

There's no getting away from the fact that it's necessary to have experience and exposure for your work by publishing individual poems before trying book publication. The reasons for this are many and varied: From establishing a reputation, to honing your craft. There is a necessary period of apprenticeship for any art form which demands focus and dedication. The writing of poetry unfortunately comes with a stock of misconceptions. Writing is a major part of communication, and we do it from an early age. Writing our feelings can come quite naturally, and we can lose sight of the fact that poetry is also an art form which demands that one is able to strike an intelligent balance between deeply felt experience and the rational, critical ability necessary to craft the experience into Poetry.

As with any art, there are people who derive great pleasure from their creativity for its own sake. There are people who make poetry for their own pleasure and don't want to go further. This is all part of what poetry means to us. However, if one aims to become professional and be taken seriously as a poet, one must go beyond the emotional high of creating. Insight is wonderful and necessary for a full life, but in poetry it has to blend with craft and originality.

We must all be very honest with ourselves about what we want for our poetry, our creativity. Above all never assume that your inner life is the only Truth. Catharsis is liberating, yes; then the work begins. Take the necessary steps to finely tune your writing – shaping it into an original piece.

3. I have a collection of short stories and poems which I am looking to have published.

Always look at the publisher's list. We don't publish short stories.

4. I am hoping to submit a poem I recently wrote. If you could read it, give me some advice, and the name of a publisher you think I could get published with.

5. My first collection of poetry is now complete but I need a grammar/punctuation expert or editor to read through them for me. Can you advise me re: who I can approach, the typical fee, and the time frame involved.

6. I have a lot of poems and I wonder if you would like to read them.

7. I would like to know who I can contact to see if my work is good enough for publication. Some of my poems are being published with poetry.com. I would like to publish my own book of poems. If you have any information I would appreciate it.

4, 5, 6, and 7 are related and I'll remark on them as one question:

A book publisher is the LAST place to seek such advice. Remember book publishers only want to see manuscripts in the final stage of their development when the poets have already gained publishing experience. A good poets' website, such as poetryireland.ie, is set up to deal with general queries, and one can find critiquing services. Editors simply don't have time to give advice on manuscripts in general.

As it happens, I do care but I still can't give detailed advice on individual poems or help people find publishers. There is added difficulty for poets since it is virtually impossible to find a literary agent who will take on a poetry manuscript. It can be a challenge to find honest, professional, advice. If one has access to a good writers' workshop, that's a start for learning critical skills. *The Writers' Handbook, Poets' Market*, and many other handbooks like these, give detailed advice and list outlets. *Poets and Writers* magazine is also an excellent source. It comes down to taking yourself seriously as a poet and doing the research!

As for publishing with poetry.com, again, my advice is to do some research. You should avoid companies that send you glowing responses to your poetry submissions; that offer easy publication in return for money; that require that you buy books, or pay for a trip to an "Awards Ceremony". Invariably they are vanity publishers and are not recognized in the literary community. It may be great to get easy praise, but think carefully about what you really want for your work, and remember that you should never pay anyone to publish your work.

8. *I basically want to know if these poems are any good.*

9. *I have lost the desire to write. Hopefully if you think the following are any good, it will persuade me to write more.*

Never, Never, Never put your creativity on the line like this. NO ONE can make decisions about your writing but you. No one can look at your writing and decide whether you should express yourself or not. ONLY YOU can sustain your writing. If you feel stuck, agree to allow yourself a little time each day for writing, and don't censor anything that comes out. Find a supportive workshop; read poetry you enjoy; browse books which give advice and writing exercises (you'll find many good ones in Online bookshops) make time to relax each day and let your thoughts flow; make time and space for yourself. Creative work is much easier when your mind is relaxed.

10. Send guidelines

We don't have specific guidelines for manuscripts. Look at our books and read the website to see the type of work we publish. I'm very clear about Salmon's aims and what we do. If a publisher does have guidelines, you'll probably find them on their website, or they will mail them to you.

11. I have a few poems that I want to get published or sold.

Literary publishers do not pay for poems. If your book is published you will receive a royalty on books sold.

12. POEMS WITHOUT accompanying info: Not a good idea to send a poem (or two, or three) on its own (see my opening remarks).

13. I am 16 years old and have been writing poems since I was very young. Recently someone read them and told me I should get them published. If I sent some of my poems to you, could you publish them for me?

Many sensitive teenagers and children write poetry. It's an excellent way to record feelings and get in touch with your deeper self. Schools often encourage this by offering creative writing classes. As a young poet matures she/he may come to see writing is an essential part of life. At that point it's crucial to take a look at expectations. If you want to communicate with like minded people through publishing, then you must learn to analyse your work in the context of an overall plan. If you are lucky you may find a good teacher/mentor in high school or college. This, however, won't substitute for your own commitment.

I've run hundreds of workshops and seen many young people who are very talented, but devalued their work because it came so naturally to them. They want to know from others if the work is good. The trouble is, there's no way forward except to gain the critical ability yourself. Looking for literary publication before one is ready is asking for rejection.

Again, it's a matter of distinguishing between what's written for yourself as an expression of feeling, and what is a perception universally shared. Before inviting rejection by looking for confirmation in inappropriate places, look closely at what you want for your poetry and how you can build up the experience to achieve it. Be realistic; submit work to college or high school journals, or other "beginning writer-friendly" outlets. Look for like-minded people who enjoy discussing poetry; organize a poetry reading with people you know who are interested in poetry in general (not just your own work); read contemporary poetry; look at books on poetic techniques. Immerse yourself. If, after all, poetry is not your major interest, you'll turn naturally to another means of expression. Above all, avoid the upset of rejection – don't send your work to publishers who only deal with professional writers until you have a good track record.

There are many issues involved in taking a ragged thought and creating a work of art. This volume aims to lend a helping hand. If I were you, I'd take it.

Jessie Lendennie,
Salmon Poetry,
Cliffs of Moher,
County Clare,
Ireland

Seamus Cashman

(Dublin, Ireland)

Some thoughts for the aspiring poet

Poets – makers of poetry – possess and seem to reside within a parallel existence to this familiar daily walk we take: sometimes poetry illumines this reality and sometimes shadows it; yet at all times, poetry is this reality.

There are nine words I have for the poet's ego to contemplate: the first six are: imagination – vision – focus – change – tradition – community. The other three (from an Irish proverb) are: sunshine – wisdom – generosity. Nine words in all. Not so much to ask of yourself. Ask.

Another good question to put is: why, if I do not write this poem, will I be poorer? It is only important to ask the question. Answering it is neither here nor there. Move on.

The Palestinian poet, Darwish, spoke of here and there – meaning place of exile and place of home. A poet is always here and there. Indeed if you are not here and there, you are unlikely to be a poet. Here is where you find what there made for you. If you write through both, and decide your poem is worth submitting to an editor, whether that editor responds at all, or declines or enthuses, is irrelevant for now. What is important is that there is a poet here. *Public-ation* is not the first call.

Recognise and then acknowledge the poet within yourself; that is the first call; the vocation, the avocation. Only then have you given yourself (installed, in laptop terminology) the permissions necessary to be that poet and to write your poem.

So, poet, come now with your poem and the editor may recognise you. But do not expect yet acceptance of your work. It most likely will take time. Keep a bunch of envelopes, stamps and letterheads in a handy drawer; know how to present your poem on the page – it is no mystery, so stop pretending.

'It is as if to be is not enough; and that to be must also be to do.' So, – get on with it. Stop moping, my mother used to say. *Nosce te ipsum* – or as it is written over *The Matrix* Oracle's door, *temet nosce*.

It's a good life being a poet. But sometimes the poet must scrape damp autumn leaves from his/her own soles regardless of who has worn the sandals. Nobody else cares. You are alone with your poet.

Yet, being a poet is quite special, and very ordinary. Remember that. It may take a while to discover. And if in the process, you awaken to some other reality, it will have been a worth while journey too.

Recommended Reading:

Irish Poetry After Yeats: Seven Poets edited by Dr Maurice Harmon.
    First published in 1979 (Wolfhound Press)
Something Beginning with P: new poems by Irish poets
    (The O'Brien Press, 2004)

Seamus Cashman is a poet, a creative writing tutor, a publisher, and an editorial & publishing consultant. His most recent poetry collection is *That Morning Will Come: New & Selected Poems* (Salmon Poetry, 2007). Earlier collections are *Carnival* (1988) and *Clowns & Acrobats* (2000). He founded Wolfhound Press in 1974, is a Fellow of the US writers and scholars think-tank, The Black Earth Institute, and is on the Board of Children's Books Ireland. He lives in Portmarnock, County Dublin.

Reading it

Maurice Harmon
(Dublin, Ireland)

Creative Reading

Without actually realising it or thinking about it we all have rhythms and rhymes, voices and settings in our heads and these affect how we write. Everyone remembers nursery rhymes and fairy tales. We have heard particular stories – about Cinderella or Little Red Riding Hood. The more they were repeated the more we liked them. I loved the story of the little girl going through the woods to visit her grandmother and gathering flowers for her along the way. The fact that it was a wood made it more vivid for me. We lived in a wood and I imagined her going from the Ardgillan demesne where we lived to Hampton, the neighbouring demesne. She went through the Postman's Gate behind which there was a line of evergreen trees leading almost all the way to Hampton Hall where the grandmother waited, or rather the wily fox waited, disguised as the old woman. These stories have a surprising amount of drama – suspense, coincidence, trickery, defining accents, and much more.

The walk to Hampton seems to have been a favourite of my mother's. We often went there with the dog and sat in a clearing enjoying the peace and listening to the sounds of the wind, birds, or distant cattle.

Stories about children in woods suited me and there were lots of them. Jack and the Beanstalk had a greater immediacy for me than stories of sea voyages. Since we lived in a wood, cut down trees and sawed them up, the woodsman hacking at the Beanstalk to kill the giant had a persuasive feel to it.

Some of my first poems were set in the woods, one about sitting in that clearing, another about climbing its trees. Even 'The Mischievous Boy', published only last year, returned to Ardgillan, to the fox and the chickens, the dog and the trains. It included, as a kind of refrain, the song my mother had taught to me and I in turn taught to my children.

> There goes the train to Dublin town
>
> Puffing along the line
>
> See how the wheels are turning around
>
> See how the red lights shine.

The Belfast-Dublin train roared through the woods; at night sparks hurled themselves into the sky; in the war years all the windows had the blinds drawn, so all one saw were the huge sparks.

What we absorb in childhood is still with us, some of it happy, some unhappy or even frightening; much of it confusing. When we reach into the world of childhood we evoke universal experience. Furthermore, it has a strong psychic connection.

It is advisable to avoid or to get away from slavish imitations. I remember using one of Byron's poems when I was away at school to describe my sense of absence from my local town. We all do this kind of thing at the beginning, seizing upon a congenial poem or being seized by it, but it is important to find one's own voice and rhythms.

When you begin to write you find it hard to find a form, a shape into which to fit the words. I found the syllabic poetry of Old Irish helpful. Writing a specific number of syllables to each line imposed a discipline on what I wanted to say. That may seem restrictive but when you are beginning it may be useful.

On the other hand certain poems have an enviable ease and fluency. Although it is years since I looked at Robert Browning's 'Home-Thoughts, from Abroad', it has a particular resonance for me. I love the way the lines run on and on through each stanza, carrying the meaning, bearing the feeling aloft, and each stanza ending with an exclamation mark to heighten his pleasure in the country scene. The familiar rural setting is one thing. Another is the use of detail. Rhymes help, of course, but the use of specific detail is exemplary.

> the lowest boughs and the brushwood sheaf
> Round the elm-tree bole are in tiny leaf,
> While the chaffinch sings on the orchard bough
> In England – now!

Robert Frost said that like a piece of ice on a hot stove a poem should ride on its own melting and that is certainly true of this Browning poem.

But there is another kind of poem that I also keep in mind and that is the poem of worry. [Thou Art Indeed Just, Lord] by Gerard Manley Hopkins is an example. All of us are at times possessed by uncertainty; we do not know where we stand, we feel displaced and find no confirming truth. Some poets make the state of uncertainty the subject of the poem. Hopkins thinks that God rewards sinners, lets them prosper, but does not reward the poet. 'Oh', he says, 'the sots and thralls of lust' thrive whereas he, God's faithful servant, does not. He looks at nature as it flourishes in Spring, and finds renewal.

See, banks and brakes

Now, leavèd how thick! lacèd they are again

With fretty chervil, look, and fresh wind shakes

Them; birds build – but not I build; no, but strain,

Time's eunuch, and not breed one work that wakes.

Mine, O thou lord of life, send my roots rain.

That last cry is heartbreaking. Apart from the sense of a voice and a presence behind it what you also see here is the ability to hold up the momentum, not to let the ice slide, to create a little drama within the lines. We need more of that.

No one piece of advice fits all. But all of us have a core of material that may lead to the creation of a poem, heard at home, learnt at school, absorbed in reading. We need to relax into it, to let it surface and help us on our way.

Recommended Reading:

The Norton Anthology of English Literature

Maurice Harmon, Emeritus Professor of Anglo-Irish Literature at University College Dublin, is a distinguished critic, biographer, editor, literary historian, and poet. He has edited *No Author Better Served. The Correspondence between Samuel Beckett and Alan Schneider* (1998) and has translated the medieval Irish compendium of stories and poems *The Colloquy of the Old Men* (2001). He has written studies of several Irish writers, including Seán O'Faoláin, Austin Clarke, and Thomas Kinsella and edited the ground-breaking anthology *Irish Poetry After Yeats. His Selected Essays* (2006) contains articles on William Carleton, Mary Lavin, John Montague, and contemporary Irish poetry. A study of Thomas Kinsella as poet and translator, *Thomas Kinsella. Designing for the Exact Needs*, was published in March, 2008. His poetry collections include *The Mischievous Boy and other poems* (Salmon, 2008), *The Last Regatta* (Salmon, 2000) and *The Doll with Two Backs and other poems* (Salmon, 2004).

Michael Heffernan

(Fayetteville, Arkansas, USA)

Reading and Writing Poetry

I teach my students how to write poetry by getting them to read it. Sometimes to minimize the expense of a huge reading list, which I am increasingly aware of these days, I avoid ordering the ubiquitous huge costly anthologies loaded with apparatus that may nod a little toward the art of poetry while tending mainly in the direction of a whole set of literary, cultural, or outright political ideologies, uttered in a "-speak" unheard of months ago – with a few poems thrown in.

Instead, I have them buy Oscar Williams's ancient anthology, *Immortal Poems of the English Language*, which I bought at the corner drug store for 25 cents in 1957. It was first published in 1952. It is still in print exactly as Williams produced it 57 years ago. At last printing, it sold for $7.95. It begins with Chaucer, Skelton, and Anonymous, and ends with Dylan Thomas. Williams died in 1964.

Thomas's "In Memory of Ann Jones," rarely anthologized anymore, is a breathtaking example of remarkably strict iambic pentameters sweeping through a 35-line cadenza of unpredictable off rhymes ("tap/sleep," "throat/clout," "thistles/puddles," "blindly/ holy/body," "all/chapel/skull," "statue/window/hollow," "pain/stone" – and more).

Oscar Williams lets the reader find this out. Apart from his two-page Introduction's surprisingly accurate assessment of his effort as an anthologist in this particular compilation, Williams says nothing about how to read or think about particular poems, anywhere, in a book of over six hundred pages. There are no notes, no appendices of related historical or critical texts, no bibliography, no suggestions for further reading, no cd in a sleeve inside the back cover.

If my students want to write free verse, I don't need to teach them how. They will do it anyway, and they will do it as well or badly as they can. Most of them get the point. I want them to liberate themselves into the freedom that attends the metered line, whether blank or rhymed.

We start with Wordsworth's "Tintern Abbey." Then we step off to meet "Kubla Khan."

Wordsworth teaches them the line and how to use it to write a personal poem about love of home, love of peace, love of beauty, love of a beloved. It can be read as a letter to the latter (Wordsworth's sister) or as an autobiographical sketch. It is very close in spirit to the sort of thing most students are ready to write immediately, or have already written by the box load. And after reading it aloud, which we may even do, at least eventually, in chorus, the magic of the line as an instrument of invention becomes apparent. An exceptional clarity prevails while the poem opens a subject, finding entry-points for secondary materials, while a third movement makes off in a radically different direction.

The fact that "Tintern Abbey" is a classic of English poetry becomes utterly irrelevant. If we wish, we can trace a tangent back to one or two speeches from Shakespeare – "Lovers and madmen" from *Midsummer Night's Dream* (ending with "How easy is a bush supposed a bear!"), or go right for it and recite "To be, or not to be"– ; instructive options abound.

Usually, I resist. If something is about to take, I really should move on. Besides, in this instance, Samuel is in the wings.

Coleridge teaches how to discover the poem you really are creating, well past the halfway mark in writing a poem about everything else. "Kubla Khan" does not begin until Coleridge gets to "A damsel with a dulcimer / In a vision once I saw." Thirty-six lines have to pass before he finds the I. Then, a deep breath later, he turns the camera on himself, and he says, "Weave a circle round him thrice, / And close your eyes with holy dread" – the second-person entering in half a heartbeat.

I tell my students this is where you launch off into modernist invention. This poem is all about discovering what you are going to write. The poem will show you what it wants to say, if you want to let it.

And the iambic line, either all by itself in its "blank" embodiment, or combined with a rhyme scheme, fixed or free, will show you what you have to say, or rather what the poem has to say.

Never start out having something to say, I strenuously announce. Find the poem the poem is going to be. Let it find itself and show you where it is. Most great poems reveal themselves to the writer first and through the writer to the reader. They seldom shout what they're about from the outset, and hardly ever anywhere else.

When we keep saying in writing workshop "Show, don't tell," we are in fact telling the students that, but the better thing to do is to show the great poems.

At some point, inevitably, we come to Frost's "Directive." The slowly manifested woodland world, full of loss, sadness, and abandonment, gradually discovers itself as a place the poet already knew or thought he knew, from many ventures into it. This time, he finds himself getting ready to drink from a forest spring, with a vessel left by a child long dead, who used it with other children to play house. It is "a broken drinking goblet like the Grail." This is five lines from the end of a sixty-two line poem. No one gets there without entering another place that opens itself only in poetry, and nowhere else.

Before we get there, we may have to mention other kinds of drink, or talk about drugs. I have told the Coleridge story about the horrific interruption. I say it may be true, but so what? We only have Coleridge's word for it – "the person on business from Porlock" seems not to have mentioned it in his diary. Coleridge could have made the story up. As to the laudanum, we know he used it, but why could he not have simply shaken awake from his vision, and begun to write "Kubla Khan" from what he had dreamt, after falling asleep as a result of a day walking around Windermere with William? Where exactly are the drugs in Xanadu? There are tons of poppies in Keats's "Endymion," Autumn himself (in "To Autumn") is "drowsed with the fume of poppies," yet everyone talks about how much Keats loved his little sips of Claret. They like him as a wino not a druggie.

It's a subject students need to have discussed, and

dismissed. I do this not by lecturing them about the last time I took a drink, or did drugs, which would bore them to tears, but by reading them the poems that people wrote while they were completely straight, possessed by better angels, intoning the many voices of the English Language. Reading poems is how I show my students how to write them, and sometimes how to live while doing that.

Recommended Reading:

Anthony Hecht, *The Venetian Vespers* (1979).
Ron Slate, *The Incentive of the Maggot* (2005).

Michael Heffernan studied at the University of Detroit (A.B.) and the University of Massachusetts (Ph.D.). Since then he has resided mainly in Michigan, Kansas and Arkansas. He has taught the study and practice of poetry at the University of Arkansas (Fayetteville) since 1986. He has published three collections of poetry with Salmon, the most recent being *The Odor of Sanctity* in 2008. His previous books include *The Cry of Oliver Hardy* (1979), *To the Wreakers of Havoc* (1984), both recently reissued by the University of Georgia Press; *The Man at Home* (Arkansas, 1988); *Love's Answer* (Iowa Poetry Prize, 1994); *The Night Breeze Off the Ocean* (Eastern Washington University Press, 2005), along with his two earlier books from Salmon, *The Back Road to Arcadia* (1994) and *Another Part of the Island* (1999). His work has earned three fellowships from the National Endowment for the Arts (US), two Pushcart Prizes, and the Porter Prize for Literary Excellence. He and his wife, Ann, live in Fayetteville, and often spend time in Ireland. They have four grown children, three sons and a daughter.

Anne Fitzgerald
(Dublin, Ireland)

The Translatable Rhythm of Breath

"When the long Atlantic coast stretches
longer and the Pacific coast stretches longer
he easily stretches with them north and south.
He spans between them from east to west and
reflects what is between them."[1]

It is what lies between either coast; boundaries of
territories, gaps and silences, this is where true poetry is to
be found. So says Walt Whitman discussing the role of the
poet in his introduction to his 1855 edition of Leaves of
Grass. One such silent poet was Emily Dickinson, whose
voice remained almost unheard to the outside world of her
Amherst contemporaries save for a handful of poems that
were published during her lifetime. Another American
poet who explores the realms of silence in her work is
Jorie Graham in such poems as, "Self Portrait as the
Gesture Between Them." In her 1996 interview: The
Glorious Thing, with Mark Wunderlich she said that,
"Poets have always written for the people in their society

who read poetry, and for the people who will read it in the future." [2]

For Paul Valéry "poetry was a language within a language" and as such, all languages have to be learned. Reading is the key to writing. When first starting out to write it is imperative that the masters are read, re-read and revisited throughout the poet's career. "The act of reading is like playing music and listening to it at the same time, the reader becomes his own interpreter." [3] The notion of the Greek Muse on the brink of what Plato called insanity, others, preoccupations, or obsessions all culminate and constitute elements of what is often "said" are prerequisites for the state of mind that writes poetry; inspiration, and a need to write might well be another. To get to that place in ones head where poems come from is the objective of every poet when they sit down to write, each taking their own circuitous root. Often twists of poems will be heard by the poet, some resonating repeatedly in the head until written down. Sometimes these twists may be the threads or canvas of a poem, on other occasions they may remain nothing more than just twists. The linguist Noam Chomsky in his 1957 book "Syntactic Structures" examined the correlations between language and the mind, broadening the field of transformational grammar and the exploration of how sentences are made. With Chomsky's adherence to phonetics, semantics and syntax (sound, meaning and word order respectively), he pushed the possibilities of linguistic parameters into the boarders of philosophical and psychological questioning.

The Chilean poet Pablo Neruda's poem "Poetry" [4] is truly a wonderful study of the awakening of the poetic imagination, where "...Poetry arrived/ in search of me, I don't know where/ it came from, from a winter or a river." [5] Neruda's epiphany occurs in the writing of the "first faint line" [6] after which the poet "wheeled with the stars,"[7] from the act of writing their first poem. The questions as to what writing is for, the importance of choosing the right words in the right order and what the power of sentences can achieve are contained in T.S. Eliot's fourth quartet "Little Gidding."

Poets have a host of technical devices that they may choose to employ from their poetic arsenal. Prosody offers style; structure and form, diction; voice and tone, sound and meaning, alliteration, assonance, irony, imagery, colloquial dialect, symbol, rhyme, figures of speech; simile, and metaphor[8] to name but a few. Some of which will be found threaded amongst generous thematic ranges presenting themselves as modern and often innovate versions of Shakespearian sonnets, or pale imitations of Homer's "Odyssey," Milton's "Paradise Lost," Elizabeth Bishop's "A Miracle at Breakfast," or of Walt Whitman's "Lilacs Last in the Dooryard Bloom'd." It is through the choice of thematic range and linguistic inventiveness, that the poet emerges to develop a distinctive style; a sureness of voice.

Politicians have over the years invoked the voice of poets. In many cases, to elevate their stature in terms of placing their political aspirations on a more intellectually interpretive one; with a capacity to embrace the environs of a more cultural intellectualisation of themselves. From Plato to Aristotle and the Elizabethans to more recent times, three such examples come to mind, John F. Kennedy (1917-1963), William J. Clinton (1946-), and Barack H. Obama (1961-). On January 20th 1961 Robert Frost was due to read "Dedication" commissioned for Kennedy's inauguration, but temporary snow blinded by the sun's glare from the White House lawn, he improvised and recited from memory, "The Gift Outright" written in 1942. With "On the Pulse of the Morning" Maya Angelou launched Clinton as a man of all seasons in January 1993, whilst Elizabeth Alexander's 2009 "Praise Song for the Day" gives Obama to all nations.

Giacomo Leopardi the Italian poet and thinker amongst his aphorisms contained in "Thoughts" talks extensively of the writers' ego and his/her inexhaustible need for an audience at any cost.[9] Nonetheless the benefits of attending a poetry reading far out weigh those for not doing so. Not least of which that when in the privacy of re-reading poetry from the text, it is possible to hear again, the voice of the poet resonating, to hear where the stresses fall. But to get to this point, new poets must find their way. After the first poems are written, the litmus test of their peers awaits. Often a way of achieving this is to seek out local arts communities, i.e. writers groups and or community arts schemes or organisations.

One such community arts organisations is Bray Arts, www.brayarts.net. which is located in Bray, Co. Wicklow and was founded in 1996. It is administered by a voluntary committee. Bray Arts is a forum for both professional and emerging artists across all artistic disciplines. One of its central objectives is to promote and develop the idea that art is for everyone in the community. And in so doing it provides a platform for artists to perform, present or exhibit their work in a supportive and appreciative environment. Formats for doing so are though the Bray Arts Journal or at one of its Monthly Arts evenings which run from September to June, where a variety of artists perform, usually from a selection of three categories: visual arts, literature and music. Though a networking development of these artistic categories both at home and abroad Bray Arts, whilst having a parochial resonance does in fact have an international audience both at its Arts evenings an in its Journal. Which is read on both sides of the Santa Fé and Oregon Trails, in New York, the Everglades, London, Paris, India and New South Wales amongst others.

Poetry can illuminate, enhance and enrich readers'

sensibilities and appreciation of what language can and might do; it can challenge traditional interpretations, and ultimately transport readers to the realms of uncharted waters. For the most part, good poetry contains a spiritual element that can transcend, transporting the reader to an elsewhere; to "...places where a thought might grow – "[10] It is in that elsewhere that the intangible becomes tangible. It is that niggling desire to touch that intangibility, as if the rub of the relic, that returns the reader again and again to a good poem. Poetry is about finding the extraordinary in the ordinary; it is like playing chess without the board. Poetry should like jazz, transport its readers to an elsewhere, but always return them home. If the origins of poetry are to be found in music and song, then lyricists such as Paul Brady, Tom Waits, and Leonard Cohen must rate amongst the list of contemporary poets.

If as Shelley asserts, Poets are the unacknowledged legislators of the world, know that there is no true legislature that can imbue the magic of where poems come from, other than what is gifted. And so, poetry it not something one fits into living; it is a way of life in which one lives, with a facility to assemble all other ancillary appendages of living to its translatable rhythm of breath. For, "Now I make a leaf of voices – for I have found nothing mightier/than they are,..."[11]

Recommended Reading:

Seferis, George, *Collected Poems* (London, Anvil Press, 1982)
Merwin, W.S., *Migration: New and Selected Poems* (Washington, Copper Canyon Press, 2005)

Anne Fitzgerald read Law at Trinity College, Dublin, and holds an MA in Creative Writing from Queen's University, Belfast. Her poetry collections are *The Map of Everything* (Dublin, Forty Foot, 2006) and *Swimming Lessons* (Wales, Stonebridge, 2001). She has edited, produced and designed four anthologies of young adults' poetry: *The Colour of the World* and *The Compass* (Dublin, MET Press, 2003, 2004); *Uncharted Voyage* and *Deep Canyons* (Dublin, Loreto Abbey Dalkey Press, 2004, 2005). She founded MET Press and Loreto Abbey Dalkey Press. She is a recipient of the Ireland Fund of Monaco Writer in Residence residential Bursary at The Princess Grace Irish Library in Monaco.

NOTES:

[1] Whitman, Walt, *Selected Poems 1855-1892*, An New Edition, ed., Schmidgall, Gary, *Leaves of Grass* 21, (NY, St. Martin's Press/Stonewall Editions, 2000), p.4. Lines 46-50.

[2] The Glorious Thing: interview appears in the Fall 1996 issue of *American Poet*, the biannual journal of the Academy of American Poets. Copyright © 1996 by The Academy of American Poets.

[3] Atwood, Margaret, *Negotiating With The Dead*, (London, Virago Press, 2008), P.44.

[4] Neruda, Pablo, *Love*, (London, Harvill Press, 1995), p.13.

[5] Ibid.

[6] Ibid.

[7] Ibid, p.15.

[8] Parini, Jay, *Robert Frost a Life*, (New York, First Owl Books Edition, 2000), p.256 on Metaphor.

[9] Leopardi, Giacomo, *Thoughts*, (London, Hesperus Press, 2002), p.17.

[10] Mahon, Derek, *A Disused Shed in Co. Wexford*, Collected Poems, (Co. Meath, Gallery, 1999), p.89.

[11] Whitman, Walt, *Selected Poems 1855-1892*, An New Edition, ed., Schmidgall, Gary, Leaves of Grass 21, (NY, St. Martin's Press/Stonewall Editions, 2000), p 200.

Lex Runciman

(Oregon, USA)

Why Do That?

I don't write poetry for money – that would be foolish. I don't write poems as a sport (bowling, basketball) or as a hobby (woodworking, macramé), though I think aspects of sport and hobby play their roles. Adam Kirsch (in the November, 2008 issue of *Poetry*), says poets write "for recognition." Grey Gowrie, in Dennis O'Driscoll's compendium *Quote Poet Unquote*, suggests "the reward is that elusive, extraordinary rightness no other art achieves" (p. 271). Two pages later, Jeanette Winterson calls poetry "a practical art. It's as good as a knife for cutting through the day's rubbish." And Pat Boran, in what is surely a grand assertion, says "The world consigns its myths, its religions, its dreams and deepest feelings to poetry for safekeeping: and, somehow, even its critics and doubters know where to find it in time of need" (p. 15). These writers are accurate, each and all. Yet.

Yet my own view is that a writer's earliest convictions about writing are at once prosaic and so deeply held as to be hardly uttered at all. Of these, the first has to do with writing as an activity, if not, early on, as craft. This occurs to you: "maybe I can do that; I've been reading (or listening) — I think I can do that; I going to try." The second follows immediately — these understandings hold hands: "my experience isn't exactly the experience I've read." Put these together and you soon get a third conviction: "I'm the only one who can write my experience, my thinking, my imagining." Phrased that way, this third conviction sounds grander than it feels at the time. What you know (maybe what you keep knowing) is that there's some promise of personal reward that will come to you if you only get the right words in the right order. When you do that — and you're the first one to read them, once you do, even if it's only a phrase or a couple of lines — the result is a clarity and an excitement that need not be compared to anything else.

I write poems because the process has the potential to teach me something about experience, including those parts of it shared with other people, including those parts of it shared with no one. My experience of time (hardly unique) is that it passes quickly, that I miss much of what goes on, much of what happens, and that I often feel experience only partially (and often understand even less). It's as though my own days pass but often I don't get what happens in them. Some days, I suppose that failure is just fine. I suppose these must just be dull days with no particular need for imagination or memory. If one believes in dull days. The time and the experience pass, and so goodbye.

In contrast, when I read a good novel or a poem that speaks to me, the first thing I do is read it again. I know there's more; I don't get it all. This knowing-I-don't-get-it-all holds the promise that if I read again I might get it, or I might get more of it. So I read again. Then again later. For a time, these works (Dylan Thomas's "Fern Hill," Elizabeth

Bishop's "The Fish," Yeats's "Lake Isle of Innisfree") become the reading equivalent of the art or the photographs one hangs on a wall. You hang a picture where you will see it daily – at the top of the stairs maybe. You hang it there not so you can ignore it but so you can see it, because for some reason or another it pleases you to see it.

We do the same with whatever's on the IPod or in the disc changer in the car: with some works, we listen and listen again. With poems, maybe I try to memorize what I'm hearing (I'm terrible at this, unless it's Frost's "Stopping by Woods on a Snowy Evening," a poem so relentlessly metered and rhymed that even I can memorize it). Such recurrence, such reading and return, is easy with poems because they're relatively short. I try to do it with novels, too, but the investment of time stretches to days and weeks for just one reading (as in *Moby-Dick* or *Portrait of a Lady*, when the last thing you want to do is hurry). My point is that writing a poem isn't so much different from reading one, except that the one I want to read hasn't been written by anyone else. I write the poem so that I can rewrite it, which is a kind of reading with benefits. It's this process I want.

Eventually, writing poems can become a habit, and it can become definitional in the way that habits define us (part of us, anyhow). I am the person who walks to work. I am the person who likes to wear vests in the winter. I am the person who enjoyed the effort and endorphins of jogging and still miss it (and them), though my lower back does not. I am the person who adds milk to my coffee. I am the person who reads as though reading is air and is therefore no more remarkable than breathing. I am the person who writes poems. I am the person who dries dishes when Debbie washes.

However, writing poems is a particularly rewarding habit because it differs from all other habits in one most significant way. Most habits are based in repetition; that is

44

what makes them habits. But writing a poem is never a repetition. In this, it mirrors days, which though they may seem to repeat, in fact really do not. Writing a poem is never a generic activity. Each writing of a poem – each writing towards a poem – is a process that cannot be foreseen. You know what you're doing but you don't know if you're doing it well or correctly or foolishly, except that you're giving yourself over to a process that you do not fully control and cannot quite predict. It's a walk in the dark, but each step seems to offer a bit more light. It's a leap. You do not know what it will yield, if anything. You're using imprecise tools (words), and you perversely wish to use as few of them as possible.

I write for this process because it asks me to pay attention in as many directions as I am able, and I'm never quite sure how many directions that might be or where they might go or what I might find or how I might at last use language to tell me.

Recommended Websites:

www.valpo.edu/vpr
for *Valparaiso Poetry Review*

www.paperfort.blogspot.com
for *Paper Fort*, the blog associated with Literary Arts, Oregon

Born and raised in Portland, **Lex Runciman** has lived most of his life in Oregon's Willamette Valley. Along the way, he has worked as a warehouseman, shipping-receiving clerk, and a stacker in a box mill. His newest collection of poems is *Starting from Anywhere* (Salmon, 2009). He is also the author of three earlier books of poems: *Luck* (1981), *The Admirations* (1989) which won the Oregon Book Award, and *Out of Town* (2004). He holds graduate degrees from the writing programs at the University of Montana and the University of Utah. A co-editor of two anthologies, *Northwest Variety: Personal Essays by 14 Regional Authors* and *Where We Are: The Montana Poets Anthology*, his own work has appeared in several anthologies including, *From Here We Speak*, *Portland Lights* and *O Poetry, O Poesia*. He was adopted at birth. He and Deborah Jane Berry Runciman have been married thirty-seven years and are the parents of two grown daughters. He taught for eleven years at Oregon State University and is now Professor of English at Linfield College, where he received the Edith Green Award in teaching in 1997.

Writing it

Rita Ann Higgins

(Galway, Ireland)

Toronto Interlude

How does a poem start, and how do you bring it to fruition? Who knows for sure. In my opinion how or where the poem begins has more to do with being receptive when the poem vein starts to leak thoughts slantways, or sideways, or anyway, or when ideas come with a new crispness, when words have a ping in their step, or when sounds evoke a memory that may be long forgotten.

Sometimes when I arrive at a new place, the wonder of that place takes over and my antennae are out for any creative crumbs that might be floating in the atmosphere.

About two years ago I was in Toronto giving a reading. It was my first time there. The hotel we stayed in was kind of posh, and we were delighted with the comfort. When we went out for a walk the most striking thing we noticed was that most of the people we saw nearby were struggling in one way or another.

The doorman at the hotel had a comic way about him. His body movements were swift, yet he would stop mid-step and change direction; a bit like Groucho Marks. His eyes darting, he had every direction scanned. He seemed to bounce when he walked; he did a kind of pirouette. He always had a wad of money that he spread out like a fan in front of his face (he wouldn't do that in parts of the Galway I know and love!). It was a peacock display thing, as if to say "I'm Flash Harry, look at me".

We got the distinct impression that Flash Harry did not like us. We were not nice luggage people, we had no Gucci labels, and we were haversackers. When we needed information about anything we were told "Ask the concierge".

Every time we went out we saw the same people – strung out or scarred by poverty, or some other sadness. It was like walking down the avenue of loss.

When I got back to Ireland the people I had seen in Toronto near the hotel, and the concierge, were jostling for position in the alleyways of my mind. They were side by side, yet Niagaras apart. A poem was starting, or a couple of lines were colliding and they would not go away. It was up to me to follow it through or let it go.

When I start writing a poem I'm not worried if the first draft does not have a sense or structure about it; it's just to get the bare bones down. It doesn't take much shape until around the third or fourth draft. By then I have a fair idea what I'm after.

I'm pleased when I get what I think is a good line. If the opening stanza is not as strong as other stanzas, I start writing it out again. Punctuation has always been problematic for me, I try not to have too many full stops because they are so sudden, and they halt things and I like the rhythm to go from the start to the end, and full stops play puck with the rhythm.

I had never seen a black squirrel before and they were plentiful in Toronto. I put 'black squirrels galore' in the notebook, I might be able to tie it in someway. (Having loads of notes won't make you ready, but notes can prompt you about things you have forgotten. So, yes, the notebook is important.)

"Some poems write themselves," the soothsayers say. I don't believe that. Poems have to be worked on, until you have done as much as you can to make all parts of the poem seem like a seamless piece.

Reading other people's work is very important, not just for the pleasure but for learning about technique and style. Put the odd poem in the rubbish bin – it's tough but it's humbling to know that not all your poems will make the final cut.

I usually find when I have lost all interest in the poem, then it's finished. This generally happens after I have been rewriting and tinkering with it for about two weeks.

It's a combination of the gut, the heart, the mind, the notebook – then the hard work starts.

Ask the Concierge

The demented walk tricky step here
jittery footfall, fractious jibe.
They bicker in the 'everything for a dollar shop.'
Later when the energy is spent
they sit with their own selves
their underweight psyche.

One begs outside a shop called 'seduction'
underwear to raise the titanic
healthy looking mannequins with brazen breasts
balefulls of Canadian promise.
They come hither you but you never come hither them.
Their chilling look deceptive, their cherry lips,
kiss me kiss me, but only in your dreams loser.

Further down the street of the black squirrel
a shop owner boasts about the underground,
you should see our underground
safest in the world, no one ever gets plugged here.
In a doorway above Hades, a policeman tells a man with no legs,
my name is zero tolerance, have you a license for that rig?
My name is zero tolerance, where is your mud guard?

The concierge has the real power here
he takes one look at your luggage, one look at you
haversacks disgust him, owners and trainers of haversacks
    disgust him more.
Cross him and you will never see one drop of Niagara fall.
He wide steps and side eyes you,
in his loose suit, hair oil up his sleeve,
his feet are made of sponge.
He deals in looks and eyebrow raising
the Concierge code, uncrackable to the luggage losers.

Back down on Loss Avenue
I ask the man outside 'seduction' if I can take his picture.
Don't ask me, I have no picture to give or take,
what you see is what you get, you see nothing you get less.

What the concierge seeks he finds
he pirouettes, he plucks, he spins, he flies
where the concierge lives, the beggar dies.

Recommended Reading:

Against Forgetting: Twentieth-Century Poetry of Witness,
    edited by Carolyn Forche (W.W. Norton)
Being Alive: The Sequel to "Staying Alive", edited by Neil Astley
    (Bloodaxe Books)

Rita Ann Higgins was born in 1955 in Galway, Ireland. She divides her time between Galway City and Spiddal, County Galway. Her first five collections were published by Salmon: *Goddess on the Mervue Bus* (1986); *Witch in the Bushes* (1988); *Goddess and Witch* (1990); *Philomena's Revenge* (1992); and, *Higher Purchase* (1996). Bloodaxe Books published her next three collections: *Sunny Side Plucked* (1996); *An Awful Racket* (2001); and *Throw in the Vowels: New & Selected Poems* in May 2005 to mark her 50th birthday. Her plays include: *Face Licker Come Home* (Salmon 1991); *God of the Hatch Man* (1992), *Colie Lally Doesn't Live in a Bucket* (1993); and *Down All the Roundabouts* (1999). In 2004, she wrote a screenplay entitled *The Big Break*. In 2008 she wrote a play, *The Empty Frame*, inspired by Hanna Greally, and in 2008 a play for radio, *The Plastic Bag*. She has edited: *Out the Clara Road: The Offaly Anthology* in 1999; and *Word and Image: a collection of poems from Sunderland Women's Centre and Washington Bridge Centre* (2000). She co-edited *FIZZ: Poetry of resistance and challenge*, an anthology written by young people, in 2004. She was Galway County's Writer-in-Residence in 1987, Writer-in-Residence at the National University of Ireland, Galway, in 1994-95, and Writer-in-Residence for Offaly County Council in 1998-99. She was Green Honors Professor at Texas Christian University in October 2000. She won the Peadar O'Donnell Award in 1989 and has received as several Arts Council of Ireland bursaries. Her collection *Sunny Side Plucked* was a Poetry Book Society Recommendation. She was made an honorary fellow at Hong Kong Baptist University in November 2006.

Emily Wall

(Juneau, Alaska)

Writing from Alaska

Publishing is a bit like starting a love affair. There are millions of sexy little literary journals and presses out there, so the question is, how do we find the right one? My experience with publishing poetry is that it's all about finding the right match.

For me, in the beginning, publishing was like blind dating. I just flung poems out there to see who I could attract. As you can imagine, this is not a terribly successful way to publish. I finally realized that while writing poems is a wholly creative act, publishing is an entirely analytical one.

Publishing a book really starts with publishing poems in literary magazines. In my experience an editor is much more likely to read your manuscript with care if they see you have a list of previous publications. I published 21 poems from my first manuscript in 18 literary journals before I submitted the manuscript to Salmon Poetry. I know fiction writers are much more likely to leap into a Vegas wedding-chapel marriage with a publishing house, but poets don't tend to work this way, nor do poetry editors tend to want this type of relationship. So, we begin with journal publications.

I set up a system for myself, and in the past 10 years I've published in over 50 literary journals using this system. I set myself the goal of sending out 10 poems a year. To reach this number, I write hundreds of poems. Twice a year I send out 5 poems to around a dozen journals. I use Poet's Market to select the journals I think best fit my work. I've found this to be an invaluable tool: Poet's Market (online as well as in print) summarizes hundreds of journals and what they are looking for. I learned early on that this is the most important step in the process; you have to know what type of work the journal likes before you submit. This is really a matchmaking exercise: if they publish only sci-fi and you're writing nature poetry, you've wasted a stamp. The best way to know a journal is to find a copy and read it, but for me, living in a very isolated community in Alaska, most small literary journals aren't available through the library or bookstores. My meager poet's budget doesn't allow me to order copies of all the journals I'd like to submit to. Fortunately Poet's Market has proved to be a useful substitute.

Once you start publishing, you'll begin to find certain journals that really like your work, and then you'll be off and running. There are a few journals that always take my work, and so I submit to these regularly. This kind of long-term relationship is lovely for both the writer and the editor.

Once you have a number of poems published, take a look at your manuscript. Does it really feel ready to become a book? If so, then you start your second round of serious research. How do you find a book editor? This works on the same principle as journal publishing, except the stakes are higher. You don't want to fling your 80 pages out into the wind and hope one of them lands in the lap of someone who likes your poems. Poetry editors are notoriously inundated with manuscripts and most of these are not published. What you want to do is find the right match.

In this case, I find buying and reading books to be the most helpful. As a poet you should already have a good library of poets whose work you admire. Start by looking at who publishes them. Then do some online research on the presses. Do they accept unsolicited manuscripts? What do their website guidelines say? Look at writers in particular whose style or themes are similar to yours.

A good place to begin is to read your regional poets. Who is writing in your particular area? Who is publishing them? Some publishers are interested in publishing the work of a particular region. I found Jessie Lendennie and Salmon Poetry through another Alaskan writer. Tom Sexton is a former poet laureate of Alaska and I had liked and read his work for years. When I got ready to send out a manuscript, and began the research process to find an editor, I saw that his most recent book had been published by Salmon. By doing some initial research online, I discovered that Jessie had a particular interest in Alaskan writers. To date, she's the only publisher I've found who focuses on poets in Alaska. This felt like a good match to me! I mailed her a partial manuscript and then came that happy day when she emailed me back, asking to see the whole book. This is the moment we poets dream about, the "yes" that comes from a book editor we admire.

So in the end, although poetry writing may begin with a glass of red wine and a symphony, publishing is all about the hard work of research. Do your research, and you'll save yourself a lot of heartache. Remember that a rejection from a press doesn't mean your work isn't worthy, it just means that press isn't the right match for you and your poems.

Recommended Reading:

Mary Oliver, *Thanks*

Robert Hass, *Human Wishes*

Emily Wall is a poet and visiting professor of creative writing at the University of Alaska Southeast in Juneau. She did her undergraduate study at Colby College in Maine and earned her M.F.A. from the University of Arizona. In 2002 she took an extended leave from Juneau and moved to British Columbia where she taught at UBC and lived on her 37' sailboat. She is currently editing a manuscript of poems that reflect her life living aboard and cruising the coast of British Columbia and Southeast Alaska. Emily has been published in a wide variety of literary journals and has won several poetry prizes. Her first book, *Freshly Rooted*, was published in 2008 by Salmon Poetry. She has also had work published in several anthologies, including poems in the recently published book *Salmon: A Journey in Poetry 1981-2007*. She has given many public readings, including a reading last year at the Bowery Poetry Club in New York City's Greenwich Village. Emily is also the faculty advisor and editor for the Southeast Alaska literary journal *Tidal Echoes*.

Susan Millar DuMars

(Galway, Ireland)

What's the Point?

I get asked this question every semester, but rarely in so straightforward a manner:

"What is the point of poetry?"

She was a young mother, and a kick-ass fiction writer, who drove an hour in each direction to come to my evening writing classes. An hour! In the dark and the rain, her homework sliding around on the backseat, to get to this overheated fluorescent-lit room. Lilliputian desks. Two vending machines dispensing the only refreshments. And she was paying for this privilege – as were the other nineteen people in the room. I owed them more than a glib answer.

But what *is* the point of poetry?

A lot of us finish school believing that poetry has no point, aside from confusing and irritating us. We've spent hours untangling ornate phrases with weird words like "thee" and "o'er" in them. Plus mind-numbing "June/croon/moon". Only to discover that it's all about some flowers in a field, and how they reminded the poet of God or dead soldiers or some chick who cut him loose. (And who could blame her? Why can't he just get to the point?)

If you are learning about writing because you want to write a novel (maybe you have a story to tell, maybe you harbour a desire to hear your name spoken by Oprah or Richard and Judy), it's hard at first to see why poetry is relevant to your studies. Yet it is. Poems have a lot to teach us about brevity and specificity; the power of an authentic voice; the joyful jolt of a brand new metaphor; the importance of the sound, the texture of language; the raw material that is our own lives.

More than anything else, to write poetry is to begin to discover the meditative mindset that good writers must achieve. It is to slow the world down, to experience as if for the first time what cold morning air actually feels like against the skin. And how that first sip of coffee really tastes. What is the exact sound your husband makes when he nicks himself shaving? What is the precise word for the smell of bread toasting? What happens behind your eyes, inside your throat when you first see the newspaper photo of the bloodied toddler in Gaza? Of these experiences we build poetry. We also, if we are lucky, build compassion, wisdom and a sense of our place in the world. Our importance, and our lack of importance. What perfect preparation for sharing our stories.

The reason the poems you were taught in school are full of archaic phrases is that the poets who wrote them lived a very long time ago. One thing is certain: They used the modern expressions of their time (some were even daring trail-blazers). We are inheritors of their creative spirit, but we don't need to use their "poetic" language. Poets writing now should immerse themselves in the world around them. The Irish poet Rita Ann Higgins opened up the world of poetry for Irish women in the mid-1980s. Her subject matter and style showed that it was OK, even exciting, to describe the everyday world – whether sitting on a bus in

Mervue, Galway, or battling with the rent man! For the modern chick's perspective, try also British poet Kate Clanchy or, from Derry, Colette Bryce.

If you'd like to know about poetry full of anger and provocation, check out Diane Di Prima's *Rant*. Or the black poet Langston Hughes' *I, too, sing America*. If you want to be shown poetic structure that is playful, and far from Shakespearean sonnets, look for the Beat poet Lawrence Ferlinghetti. If you want proof that human experience rendered in colloquial language can affect a reader like a knee to the stomach, please read Irish poet Dennis O'Driscoll's *What She Does Not Know Is*. After you catch your breath, ask me again the point of poetry.

Don't stop there. Gorge yourself on modern poetry; then turn back to those poems you learned in school. Bring patience. Bring a dictionary. Bring the knowledge that it is okay not to know, to have questions. Let these older pieces slowly reveal to you what it was like to be alive a hundred years ago. Two, three, four hundred years. Then smile when you realize it wasn't all that different from life today. Celebrate, and bemoan, the unchanging nature of human existence.

This is what we do in class; dissect newer poems, then older ones. Celebrate and bemoan. Then, to prove to students that their own worlds are worth writing about, I ask them to write a poem in the form of a letter to a member of their family. They must read the resulting poem to the class. Most students start this reading by apologising for their poor effort. Then they read, and learn from the rapt attention and excited responses of their classmates that they've created a poem that works; it reaches people and moves them. The reason they couldn't recognize the value of their own piece is that they have written the same way they speak. They are used to their own speech and don't see anything interesting about it, but to the rest of us that voice is a revelation. This is why a writer seeking a "new" style with which to dazzle the critics should look within. Only you can write like you! As long as you are true to yourself your work can't help but be fresh and persuasive.

We sometimes follow this with the 'Body of Water' exercise. (I did not invent this one; I learned it from poet John Walsh, who may well have learned it from someone else). Each student starts a poem with the line *I am an ocean* – or lake, or puddle, or fountain, whatever body of water they choose. They then write about themselves by writing about the water. They are deep, cold, restless, reflective, and so on. This assignment goes to the heart of metaphor, which is the description of something familiar accomplished by comparison to something unexpected. The spark made by rubbing the known against the new is what sets poetry, and all good writing, ablaze. It is the writer's job to see the ordinary in an extraordinary way.

A lot of myths have grown around the art of writing poetry. Here are the myths I debunk every semester:

1. A poem should be written in one go.

Actually, most published poems have been through several drafts. Many poets take advice from editors, teachers and fellow poets in refining their work.

2. If it doesn't rhyme, it isn't a poem.

Much modern poetry does not rhyme. It is compression – every word absolutely necessary – married to musicality – an ear for the sounds of words – resulting in the evocation of emotion that makes a poem a poem.

3. Poems should contain a lot of high-flown abstractions, like *love, justice, fate.*

Wrong! The most effective poems stick with the specific and concrete, engaging the five senses of the reader.

4. Form and content are not related.

In fact, tension between the two can give a poem power. For example, you may find it easier to explore raw emotions in a tightly structured poem. The rhyme scheme, stanza length, etc. will act as a container for unwieldy feelings.

5 Titles are not important.

A title can grab a reader's attention, contextualize a poem, establish a recurring phrase or motif, and/or take some of the weight off that first line.

6. A real poet is unconcerned with the material world; she lives and works in isolation, drinks a lot, and has nothing to do with promoting her own work. Genius will find an audience.

Well…**no**. First of all, as I've said, the material world is the poet's subject matter. Ideas come from contact with life, in all its messiness.

Drinking a lot is expensive and generally leads to decreased productivity (and if she spills cabernet on her laptop she's screwed!).

There is little money in poetry, and that means agents (who need to make a living, after all) aren't interested in representing poets. Poetry publishers tend to be under-funded and overworked. So if the poet wants her work read, she had better submit it to magazines, websites, competitions and publishers herself. She will need to present her work at readings as well. Genius is nice; hustle is important too.

That is, of course, if you do want your poems read by the public. Maybe you don't. Maybe you write them for your children and grandchildren, so they will know how life looked to you. Maybe you write them for your partner, so even if you find it hard to say it aloud he will know how very much you love him. Maybe you write poems for your God, to celebrate His work or to ask Him questions you don't dare ask in prayer. Maybe your poems are for you, alone; a way to give concrete form to nebulous emotions. To put your footprints in the sand.

All of these are good reasons. For me, the point of poetry is to give me back my life. I'm always losing bits of it – to forgetfulness, to busyness, to cowardice too. When I write a poem I am brave and I am still. And my memory stretches back like thousands of miles of scenic road. When I write a poem I own my life.

And that, my friends, is the point.

Recommended Reading:

Satan Says by Sharon Olds (University of Pittsburgh Press, 1980).
The Writer's Voice by Al Alvarez (Bloomsbury Publishing, 2005).

Susan Millar DuMars is an American writer who has lived in Galway, Ireland for eleven years. Her debut poetry collection, *Big Pink Umbrella*, was published by Salmon Poetry in 2008. A follow-up collection, *Dreams for Breakfast*, will appear in 2010. Susan enjoys reading for audiences, and has performed in literary events in the US, Britain, Greece and Ireland. Susan also writes fiction, and in 2005 received an Irish Arts Council bursary for her short stories. *American Girls*, a mini-collection of eight stories, was published by Lapwing in 2007. She is currently working on her first full short fiction collection. Susan teaches creative writing to adults, children and special needs groups. She and her husband Kevin Higgins have run the successful Over the Edge readings series in Galway since 2003.

Joan McBreen

(Tuam, Ireland)

Getting Started

It was the autumn of 1986. I was living in Tuam, County Galway with my husband, Joe McBreen and our six children, then aged three to fourteen years. I was also teaching at a primary school and had little time for myself. To consider writing and publishing poetry seemed an impossibility. I had written and published poetry in my native town of Sligo as a teenager. Then in 1970 I married and started a family and the writing side of my life was, for the most part, abandoned.

My father died in October 1986 and, in some miraculous way, poetry once again found me, or I found poetry. Around that time a young girl died in Tuam. She was the second daughter of a well-known family in the town to die of cystic fibrosis. I was moved to write and publish an elegy in the local newspaper *The Tuam Herald*. The editor, David Burke soon became a friend of mine. He was aware of Jessie Lendennie and her then husband, Michael Allen, who were involved in The Galway Writers' Workshop. He encouraged me to go along to this group, which met weekly in Galway.

The first time I met Jessie was in the downstairs bar of the late Mick Taylor's pub. There she was, warm and welcoming, surrounded by two large dogs and a couple of flamboyantly dressed people. One was a young Irish-American woman, the poet Nuala Archer. The other older woman was the photographer and poet, Anne Kennedy. Anne was from California, but she had been living in Galway for some years.

Jessie led us up the stairs and into a large and quite dark family dining-room. Around a mahogany table sat a group of men and women. I was introduced to Rita Ann Higgins, Eva Bourke, Eoin Bourke, Michael Allen, Moya Cannon, Mary Dempsey and others whose names escape me at the moment. Poems were being read and shared with the group and critical comments flew over and back across the table. I was petrified and completely out of my depth! To my astonishment I found, that when I made eye contact with Anne Kennedy she was almost in tears. What a start!

On the twenty mile drive back to Tuam I found myself thinking that I could not and would not ever have the courage to face into such a situation again. But as the subsequent days wore on my thinking changed and I was back at Taylors the following week.

Anne Kennedy and I struck up a friendship. After the second workshop session that we attended, we sat over Anne's Aga stove at her house in Ballinfoile Park in Galway and began to share our life stories. This was to be the beginning of one of the most rewarding and important friendships of my life. It was a great loss to me and to Ireland's literary life when Anne died, prematurely, in 1998. Anne and I had a subconscious understanding. We both knew we had stories to tell and poems to write, but neither of us had a clue how to go about it. But we were smart enough to recognise that this group of writers and poets that we had been fortunate enough to encounter, knew a lot more than we did!

We both resolved to try to crack this mystery or, as Jessie kept saying at the Workshop, "find your own voice". I wrote my poems, Anne wrote her poems and suddenly, at one of the workshops, Jessie said she liked what we were writing and that she would like to publish some of them in the little magazine she and Michael Allen were editing *The Salmon Magazine*. When my poem "My Father" appeared in print for the first time I almost cried with joy. But more than that, the affirmation made me even more determined that writing and publishing my poetry would become the centre of my life. To even begin to describe the difficulties this was to create for me as a wife and mother would be the subject of a much longer essay than the one I am engaged in writing now.

In those heady, early days of the Galway Writers' Workshop, for the first time in my life, I knew I had found new friends, and new certainties. Sometimes one or more members of the group would make it very clear that a poem of mine was not up to scratch and I would almost drown in a sea of self-pity. But then I would go home to Tuam and begin all over again.

One evening, I learned at the Workshop and from the local media, that Eavan Boland, a poet whose work I had always admired, was giving a reading in Galway city. I had no babysitter. In order to attend the reading I had no choice but to bring my six young children with me. I piled them all into a yellow Volkswagen (no fancy child seat-belts or SUVs in those days!) and off we went. At the end of the reading I braved it up to Eavan and very shyly asked her, " how is it possible to be a mother and a poet"? To this very day I can still see the tears in her eyes as she looked at me and at the children who were gathered around me. It was to be many years before I knew what those tears of hers meant. Eavan invited me to join a series of workshops she was giving at that time at the Irish Writers' Centre in Dublin. I can't remember how I managed to attend, but attend I did. Then I knew that the encouragement and the practical advice that I and many other women poets, received from poets like Eavan and Jessie was unique. This, after all, was the Ireland of the late 1980s and the early 1990s with all the social and cultural injustices suffered by Irish women, now well-documented in books such as *The Transformation of Ireland* by historian, Diarmuid Ferriter. This book, together with the work of another very well-known historian, Dr. Margaret MacCurtain, will enhance and inform readers who wish to know more about the period I write of here.

I do remember Eavan Boland telling us the story of the woman she encountered at a workshop she was giving somewhere in the midlands of Ireland. Eavan was, if my memory serves me well, trying to tell this particular woman that her poems were good and that she should try to have them published. The woman said in a horrified voice that this would be impossible because, if she published her poems her neighbours would think she never washed her windows!

When I'm asked for advice by emerging poets I emphasise two things. Firstly, I believe strongly in the value of the workshop, even with its possible "dangers". Secondly, I believe in perseverance. Of course, life and its events will do its best to throw even the most determined and talented poets off track. The Muse is fickle and does not like to be ignored. It can be very difficult for the poet to humour Her again, after having been forced, for whatever reason, to abandon her! All poets will have this experience from time to time, but staying on course is essential for the development of the poet's work and for ultimate success.

An aspiring poet who decides to attend a workshop lead by an established poet should become familiar with the work of that poet. Likewise, when sending work out to magazines and literary journals, it is wise to read issues of the publications and know their tone and interests.

In my experience, poets can gain a lot by attending literary festivals and enrolling in poetry workshops, for example, The Yeats Summer School, Sligo or Listowel Writers' Week, Co. Kerry. The organisers of these festivals and of many others are very careful to invite well established poets to lead workshops. They ensure that workshop leaders are sensitive to the needs of younger and less established poets and writers. Much confidence is gained by being in the same environment as others who are anxious to develop their craft and are serious about it.

The practical aspects of getting published are always given due attention at these workshops. Another great advantage of attending literary festivals is the friendships that are formed between people with similar passions and interests. On a personal note, I remember with much affection the late Seán Dunne and a workshop of his that I attended years ago in Listowel. His shining spirit came with him each day to the workshop sessions and, all those fortunate to have encountered him carry in their hearts his advice and wisdom, together with his fine sense of what is important in the world of the poet and in his or her life. Thankfully, other mentors and workshop leaders are still with us including Tom McCarthy, Gabriel Fitzmaurice, Richard Murphy, Mark Granier, Medbh McGuckian, Eavan Boland and Nuala Ní Dhomhnaill, to name but a few. And it would be wrong of me not to mention the fun enjoyed at Clifden Arts Week, Connemara, Co. Galway, with founder and director Brendan Flynn seeing to it that everyone is acknowledged and made feel welcome. Poets,

Tony Curtis and Michael Coady have been wonderful Clifden ambassadors over the last number of years and are generous also with their time and talent.

In conclusion, for myself as a working poet, one of the most important things is to be a good reader of poetry. That includes reading those poets who are no longer 'fashionable'; for who is to know what will endure, or for how long? At the heart of all is the mystery of poetry itself.

Recommended Reading:

W.B. Yeats – *Collected Poems*
Louis MacNeice – *Collected Poems*

Joan McBreen is from Sligo and divides her time between Tuam and Renvyle, County Galway. Her poetry collections are: *The Wind Beyond the Wall* (Story Line Press, 1990), *A Walled Garden in Moylough* (Story Line Press and Salmon Poetry, 1995), *Winter in the Eye: New and Selected Poems* (Salmon Poetry, 2003) and *Heather Island* (Salmon Poetry, 2009). She was awarded an MA from University College, Dublin in 1997. Her anthology *The White Page / An Bhileog Bhán: Twentieth-Century Irish Women Poets* was published by Salmon in 1999 and is in its third reprint. *The Watchful Heart: Twenty-Four Contemporary Irish Poets: Poems and Essays*, another anthology compiled and edited by McBreen, is published by Salmon in 2009. Her poetry is published widely in Ireland and abroad and has been broadcast, anthologised and translated into many languages. Her CD, *The Long Light on the Land: Selected Poems*, read to a background of traditional Irish airs and classical music, was produced by Ernest Lyons Productions, Castlebar, County Mayo in 1994. She has given readings and talks in many universities in the USA including Emory, Villanova, De Paul (Chicago), Cleveland, Lenoir Rhynne, N.C. and the University of Missouri-St.Louis.

Together with her on-going involvement with Irish literary festivals such as the Yeats Summer School, Clifden Arts Week, Listowel Writers' Week and The Cúirt International Festival of Literature, McBreen has, since 2007, been Literary Advisor and co-ordinator of the Oliver St. John Gogarty Literary Festival at Renvyle House Hotel, Connemara, Co.Galway.

Eamonn Wall

(St. Louis, Missouri, USA)

A Delicate Balancing Act

At some point in their early development, poets-starting-out-on-their-careers will take the exciting and fateful step of emerging from the solitude of home or cafe to join the community of writers out there in the wider world. Casually, he/she will ask a friend to cast an eye over a poem, or a batch of poems will be sent in the post to a literary magazine, or the step might be taken to enroll in a poetry workshop at a college or through a community group, and it is the latter opportunity that I will be concerned with here having, over a twenty-year period conducted workshops for poets ranging in age from seven-year-olds to those in their seventies.

It has often been said of the poetry workshop that 90% of the feedback generated is useless whereas the 10% that is good and to the point is indispensable, and this seems a fair point though it is not always easy to decide which is which, particularly when the commentary provided is contradictory – as it often is. What the poet is forced to do, in order to find the nuggets in the feedback, is to think long and hard on the comments that have been provided. It is important to test the commentaries against the poem itself and, thereby, to understand that all writing is collaborative, and that readers in workshops, albeit with a wide variety of views, are vested in the project of making each poem that is read an improvement on what is was before.

The best students, both in the short and long term, are those who give generously to the workshop both in how they respond to the work of others but also in how they take into account, and wrestle with, the commentaries their own work has received. Generally, those poets who get the least from a workshop are those who give little to it because they have little or no interest in what their peers write and who ignore, or pay lip-service to, the feedback their own work has generated. Such poets will change little in their work seeing the class as an exercise in proofreading rather than substance.

Most poems, particularly those that look unforced, require a great deal of re-writing and this is something that even the most experienced poets realize and why they share their work with colleagues for the purpose of receiving useful criticism.

A long-term aim of any writing workshop is to develop in the writer an ability to read his/her own work with a degree of objectivity so that the writer, when the time comes to walk away from workshops for good, will be in a position to make sophisticated judgments as to the merits of lines, forms, images, metaphors, metres, and the diction and syntax of poems. If the writer does not take criticism seriously, it will be impossible for him/her to develop the clear and objective eye that is one of the keys to writing good poetry.

Is it necessary for poets to receive formal training in the craft in order to become good writers? Of course not. The teaching of creative writing is a recent phenomenon – for centuries writers got by without workshops and certain writers today will work better, and develop their skills more quickly, without the benefit of workshops. For most, however, the workshop will serve as an important link between the kitchen table and the literary world.

Poets will always be told that they should constantly be reading poetry to be better acquainted with the various historical traditions in poetry, and with what is going on in the contemporary scene. It is certainly true that good poets are well-read poets. However, in many instances the beginner is given little or no indication as to what he/she should read – it's as if he/she has been told by a doctor to take medicine for a condition without the actual medicine to be taken being prescribed. It is best to start with what is simplest and to use this path to lead you into the more complicated territories. All poets should read the literary magazines of their own place, should attend poetry readings and festivals, and browse in bookshops in the contemporary section to find books that are appealing. Since poetry is rooted in ancient traditions and spread across continents, the poet will soon be alerted to the work of other writers across countries and centuries and should be eager to be led into hitherto uncharted areas. When poetry is being discussed, listen carefully. If a collection by a poet you have not heard about is mentioned, write down the title in your notebook and then search for it in your local library or bookshop. Also, give some of your time each year to reading, or re-reading, from the classics.

The good poet is both curious and adventurous and will relish the challenge that new writers will present to his/her sense of what is important in poetry. Reading is often a great spur to writing, a way of getting the juices flowing, and, for some writers, a pre-requisite for getting started. And, as we all know, as we are reading we are learning even if we don't know it, and even if we hate the book we are currently reading. The poet going nowhere will insist that he/she is one of a kind, and in no need of the work of others.

It is can be very difficult for me to predict at the end of a three-month long poetry workshop the poets who will go on to have their work appear in magazines or in book form. There are many reasons for this. At times, the best writer in a group will express little interest in continuing with poetry writing when the workshop is over while another good writer, full of energy and enthusiasm while a student in the workshop, will lose interest and a sense of purpose once the workshop has ended and the group has dispersed. It can be very difficult to get one's work accepted for publication with the result that many talented poets, instead of being patient and persistent, will grow frustrated and will eventually give up. Five years down the road, it is not unusual that the best-published poet of a class is someone surprising, an individual I might have passed over in some respects, the poet who used the workshop as a starting point rather than as an end in itself. It is a reminder to me that we all learn in different ways and not a shared pace. As is often pointed out, we should always want to have our best work published while at the same time learning to separate the act of writing from that of submission so that frustration with the latter will not have a negative effect on the former. It is a delicate balancing act.

Recommended Reading:
Frank O'Hara, *The Selected Poems of Frank O'Hara*
Carol Muske, *Wyndmere*, University of Pittsburgh Press

Recommended Website:
Irish Writers On Line – www.irishwriters-online.com

Eamonn Wall is a native of Enniscorthy, Co. Wexford, who now lives in Missouri. *A Tour of Your Country*, his fifth volume of poetry, was published by Salmon in 2008. His essays and articles are collected in *From the Sin-é Café to the Black Hills* (University of Wisconsin Press). He teaches at the University of Missouri-St. Louis.

John Hildebidle

(Massachusetts, USA)

"What do you do?"

Since I teach at what proudly claims to be the foremost institute of scientific and technological study and research in the world, I've developed a little comedy routine.

> "What do you do?"
> "I'm a professor."
> "Oh? Where?"
> "MIT."
> "Oh. What do you teach?"

Now comes the moment which both Mark Twain and George Burns asserted is crucial to the effectiveness of a comic story: the pause. I can almost hear the inner workings of my interlocutor's imaginings: quantum physics? computer science? bioengineering?

> "English. Poetry, mostly."

The reaction is either a guffaw or a look of shocked disbelief. Once, I was labeled "the bravest man I know."

This for teaching poetry to engineers. It is indeed an anomalous trade, but given that the engineers are as bright as anyone their age, it hardly merits a Purple Heart.

Granted, there is a certain amount of trickery called for – especially given the widespread fear of/distaste for poetry. Of course, my students have voluntarily enrolled in my class, so I can presume that they are leaning slightly in the right way, allowing me, like a proficient in judo, to complete the transformation. Years ago, trying to devise a metaphor for what it is I do, professionally, I hit upon the notion that I am a Missionary in Humane Letters to the Overnumerate Heathen. I once had a student who turned in a late paper with an appended note, first offering predictable excuses, and then a line that won me over: "Thank you for teaching me a new way to think."

Among the lamentable number of half-mistaken lessons I learned in high school, one had to do with poems and images. A poem, so I was confidently told, was an arrangement of words that frequently (almost always, until recently) rhymed. But the heart of the poem was its image. Poems were customarily allowed only one image, and it was the job of the poet to define and manipulate that image in the cleverest fashion imaginable. Poems, in short, were more or less images with fins and chrome. This was the Fifties, so fins and chrome were compliments.

It wasn't hard to find poems that fit the definition pretty well. This concept of poetic images was one of those dangerous errors that are partly true, and therefore partly provable. Fortunately, its usefulness wears away quickly, once you escape from Ogden Nash. It doesn't do a darned bit of good with Yeats or Wallace Stevens or even Shakespeare's sonnets, which have a nasty way of piling image on top of image, of complicating verbal pictures – that's what an image is, isn't it? that's why they call it an image, just like a photograph, isn't it? – with sound patterns.

It finally dawned on me, one day (I won't say how old I was; I'm a little embarrassed to admit how long it took me to wise up) that poems were insidious little things that took as their work the complete unsettlement of the universe, the challenging of all the consoling presumptions you'd tinkered together over the years. Poems are, often in the quietest way possible (they've figured out, you're a more likely sucker if you're half asleep) complete revisions of the way you think. They have, at their disposal, a whole range of tricks, honed to a fine complexity over the centuries. But mostly they work with only two meager tools: language and imagery.

The problem with language is that it's so shopworn, used by everyone from Shakespeare to children singing nursery-rhymes. Still it has one advantage: it's always multiple. Unlike numbers, for instance, any word worth its salt (or, more to the point, worth its poem) means four or a dozen things. The poem's work is to try to unleash all of those meanings at once. Which is why poems are bad things to read when you're trying to relax yourself to sleep, and impossible things to read fast: they demand that you linger over almost every word, considering the possibilities the way chess champions are supposed to be able to do.

But language (along with its subsidiary pleasures, like sound and rhythm) is really just the raw material of the poem. What makes it a poem (as opposed, say, to a short op-ed piece) is the image. William Carlos Williams said once that:

It is difficult
to get the news from poems

yet men die miserably every day
for lack
of what is found there.

It is worth keeping in mind that Williams was not some pie-in-the-sky Pollyanna. He spent his adult life as a physician, in the slums on Paterson New Jersey. One might doubt whether his patients knew (or cared, for that matter) that he was a prolific poet. But his assertion is more plausible if you understand that the "news" a poem brings to its attentive reader is the image.

To the poet, the image – observed or imagined, or (when things are working properly) both at once – is the germ. To the reader, the image is something else. In fact, that's part of the heart of the matter: the image is something else, something unexpected, something unfamiliar, and maybe even (when the poem tackles one of those nagging Big Questions, like death or love or the nature of the universe) something unpleasant. All the poem wants you to do, after all, is look at everything – every darned single thing – in a new way. And the image is the lens it asks – no, demands that you look through (and entices you to look through, too, of course). Williams is a master of this; one of his poems demands that you look scrupulously, and in the end lovingly, at a brown paper bag being blown down a city street. Every poet has his or her favorite pallet of imagery; it's one of the things that makes for a unique poetic "style" or "voice."

But it may be with images that there are really only two kinds, the useful and the ineffective. No, not useful; necessary, the ones that nag and nag at your mind, as opposed to the ones you can't even remember, ten minutes later – the ones that change the world and the ones that just take up space. Read enough poetry and the images will stay, forming your vision. On a bright December day you will not be able to keep from remembering that:

> There's a certain slant of light,
> Winter Afternoons –
> (EMILY DICKINSON)

A month or so earlier, fighting like mad to avoid thinking of age and mortality, still there will come creeping into your mind the thought that:

> That time of year thou may'st in me behold,
> When yellow leaves, or none, or few, do hang
> Upon those boughs which shake against the cold.
> (WILLIAM SHAKESPEARE)

And once you've made it again to the grey days of earliest March, you'll look out the car window at some unprepossessing field full of the

> reddish
> purplish, forked, upstanding, twiggy
>
> stuff of bushes and small trees
> (WILLIAM CARLOS WILLIAMS)

and realize that, if you could only look hard and carefully enough you'd be able to see "the stiff curl of wildcarrot leaf" as "Spring and All" triumphs again. It's a kind of joyous madness, really, an addiction. But, gloriously enough, it's perfectly legal, and low-calorie, and guaranteed 100% cholesterol free. The best bargain going, when you come right down to it.

John Hildebidle lives and works in Cambridge, Massachusetts, where he teaches English at MIT. He is the proud father of two wondrous childen, the equally proud author of four books of poems and one collection of short fiction. Among the books he most admires are all Billy Collins's and Ted Kooser's collections, and the Poetry 180 and Writer's Almanac web sites.

Jean O'Brien

(Ireland)

Workshops

There is always a feeling of excitement when I start a new class – will I get on with everyone, will they gel as a group, are there any 'naturals' amongst them? You cannot teach anyone how to write, you can only guide, encourage and point out possibilities, Every now and again you come across someone in a group who just seems to have hit the street running. The poems seem to come easily to them, they are almost fully formed when they arrive. You find it hard to believe that this person hasn't been writing and even publishing for years.

I have met such people a few times over the years and when I do I get what I could only describe as a rush of envy; writing seems to come so effortlessly to them, they almost take it for granted. Unfortunately, often the same people who are blessed with such a gift don't realise the blood and sweat most of the rest put into our work. At least two people I knew with the gift have stopped writing altogether, which seems such a waste. I want to say, "Bless me with it – I'll make good use of it!" Irish poet Dora Sigerson Shorter said of her own work and talent, that she possessed "a slender talent well served". Some people have a greater talent, not served at all, to the impoverishment of the rest of us.

Then there are the people often met in workshops who read little, if any, poetry, but are convinced that their poems are just great and that the tutor is at fault for not understanding their brilliance. These are often people who have put very little work into their poems and resist changing even one word. They tell you, "But it really did happen, I really did feel that." My cruel-to-be-kind answer is. "I don't care if it is true or not – it has not yet been shaped into a poem." As the poet Rita Ann Higgins says, "Don't let the truth get in the way of a good story." I always tell people to revise, revise, revise.

In the early years of the Dublin Writers Workshop (a writing group that was set up in the 1980s) we sometimes had people who joined the group, but also felt threatened by it. One of these people was a young woman who objected strenuously if anyone used a word with more than four letters or one syllable. Despite myself, I became fed up with this and bluntly told her: "Buy a good dictionary." She may or may not have taken my advice, but she stuck with the workshop, improving her work as she went along and eventually went into adult education and took a degree in English at Maynooth University. This is one of the positive things about workshops – they foster development. This was certainly the case for me, and my own work.

When I start a new workshop I always try to keep in mind how I felt at the first workshop I attended. It was run by established writers Dermot Bolger and John Grundy at The Grapevine Arts Centre, Dublin. The first night I attended, people were getting up and reading their work and the others in the group were commenting. The discussion got very lively and I took complete fright and went home. I didn't pluck up the courage to go back for another six months. I wrote a poem about the experience, so at least I got something from it, but I really felt that all the other people knew some secret that I didn't. I didn't know how to take part. Over the years I have grown a protective carapace, which you need if you are to survive, but I always try to remember what it can be like for people starting out. I can't recall which writer gave this advice, but it is worth thinking about: "Don't write unless you really have to". I really had to.

A number of years ago a woman came to a workshop that I was running. She had brought a poem with her that, as she explained before she read it out, was on the sad subject of the loss of a child. Unfortunately, when she read the poem to us, it was little more than doggerel. I could not for a moment doubt her utter sincerity, but the fact was it had yet to be transformed into poetry. I tried to delicately point this out, suggesting that as she had brought it to a workshop, she could surely take a little advice about making some changes to it, such as the three beat rhyming scheme that almost had us singing. But no, obviously the subject was too raw and perhaps she had shown it to us for therapeutic reasons only. The rest of the workshop responded to the subject matter and were not having any criticism of the piece. I know when I am beat and backed off.

Some years later, the same woman presented herself at one of my workshops. To be truthful, my heart sank and I wondered how I was going to manage the situation. I was pleasantly surprised when the poem she read out was pretty good, well thought out and well-crafted. At the end of the class I told her that I found her work much improved. She told me that what I had said to her had stayed in her mind, but at the time she was just not able to use it. Then, after a few years she had started to take it on board. She had certainly put it to good effect. So to mix a metaphor; even if you think you are throwing straws to the wind, it can surprise you to see some of them seed and take root.

Recommended Reading:

The Making of a Poem, Eds. Mark Strand & Eavan Boland,
    A Norton Anthology.

Recommended Website:

The Poetry Society in the UK – http://www.poetrysoc.com/

Jean O'Brien is a Dubliner now living in the Midlands. Her work is widely published in magazines and journals. She has published three collections of poetry, *The Shadow Keeper* (Salmon,1997), *Dangerous Dresses* (Bradshaw Books, 2005), and *Lovely Legs* (Salmon, 2009). She read for an M.Phil. in Creative Writing from Trinity College and facilitates creative writing classes for venues as diverse as the Irish Writers' Centre, Dublin City Council and various County Councils and in Mountjoy, Limerick and the Midlands Prisons. She was Writer-in-Residence for Co. Laois in 2005. She was last year's recipient of the Fish International Poetry Award. Also in 2008 she was commissioned to write a poem for the Oxfam Calendar. Her poetry was described by Fiona Sampson writing in the Irish Times as "effortless writing, graceful and exact as any pirouette in its insight".

Caroline Lynch

(Galway, Ireland)

The Long Labour

I wrote my first poems when I was about seventeen. I don't know why I started writing except that I had grown up reading and took it for granted that words on a page were the best way, the only way, to express being alive, being in the world. I also wrote short stories, but over time these became less common. The poems, however, continued.

My first poems are not worth talking about except to say they were the first ones and they were written. In college, things improved a little bit. It was in college, in 1996, that I first entered a poetry competition. I won it, but was not one bit comfortable reading my poem aloud, or posing for a photo. I felt like a fake. If the judges knew that all my other poems were unintelligible drivel they wouldn't have given me the prize. The poem was put in a little stapled book. It stared up at me accusingly. Where were its brothers and sisters from my keyboard (I can't say pen) to prove I wasn't just a one hit wonder?

After college, I studied acting. I thought that this

would satisfy my love for words. My writing continued, but haphazardly. If people asked what I did, I replied I was an actor. The description 'writer' did not apply. But being alive in the world still needed to be expressed through words. In my last year of drama school my grandfather died. I wrote a poem about him, read it at his funeral and, two years later, entered it in a competition. It was short listed. The first prize was £3,000. I went home with my runner-up cheque of £100, which was just as well, because I was still a fake.

But Merrily Harpur from the Strokestown Poetry Festival was there and she asked me to come and read in Strokestown the following year, 2002. I gathered up a clutch of poems and read there, dazed by the sheer number of *poets!* People who said, openly and without embarrassment, that they wrote *poems!* Rooms with people in them, listening to *poetry!*

My acting was running out of steam. There's more than a love of words involved in acting (but more about that another time) and, in late 2003, I began a solicitor's apprenticeship. This period of steady (not large!) income, regular days and no other creative work allowed me to concentrate on writing.

I joined a creative writing class in the Irish Writers' Centre in late 2004, tutored by Nuala Ní Dhomhnaill. For the first time I was in a public space for writing that did not provoke the internal tensions of competition and prizes. We had homework and deadlines, ideas for poems and discussions about form and structure. When the 10 week course ended the work continued with the class publishing a book of its work for charity. There's no doubt that I committed the cardinal error (even sin?) of including poems that needed more time to settle. But for the first time I felt able to read my poems to people and not feel like a con. I knew I was onto something, not just for writing but for being alive.

I got a place on the MA in Writing at the National University of Ireland, Galway (NUIG) and went west in the summer of 2006. The MA was not confined to poetry, but included, among other disciplines, non-fiction, fiction and research writing. I was glad of the chance to write in other forms, wondering if I might be like the oft-quoted student who went in writing in one form and came out writing in another. But I came out still writing poetry. I got better at separating the part of me that writes from the part of me that presents my writing to the world. I got my lowest MA mark in the poetry module and then won the Listowel Writers' Week poetry collection competition. But both of these results seemed to happen to the outer part of me and didn't overwhelm the place where writing comes from.

The Listowel prize involved two trips to Co. Kerry: one in May 2007 to accept the prize and another in May 2008 to launch the resulting book. On the first trip I accepted my cheque and silver pen and, though nervous, read a few poems with an equanimity my younger self would never have believed possible. The second trip was more complicated. When I won the competition it was not guaranteed that I would have a book published. The prize included money towards publishing, but did not provide a publisher. I had to find that myself.

I finished my MA and kept writing, but it wasn't until January 2008 that I looked back through what I had written and thought maybe I should at least try to find a publisher. I got a rejection letter from one that I could only read once as it literally gave me a pain in my heart. But in some way, I felt I was finally facing down the thing I had been most afraid of, that is, being unmasked as a fake, or, as just not very good. And then the dust settled and I got back to writing again.

That letter advised me to read more. That is the other thing: *read more!* I'd heard this advice for years, and I did try to read poetry but often came away from reading a poem feeling disconnected or under-whelmed. It wasn't that the poem didn't work. My brain couldn't let the words through to the mysterious darkness that longs to be lit up. This, of course, used to make me feel incredibly hypocritical in my desire to write poems. Why was I writing them when I didn't even read them? The process (still on-going) of making me a better reader seems to involve reading less prose for quite a while, then slowly increasing the amount of poems I read, reading them aloud and also re-reading them and (sometimes) learning them by heart. Those dark places in my head flicker now; an almost physical sensation when I read a poem I like, or, if it's a poem I don't like, I can feel the darkness fill with disappointment. Either way, something's happening. Poems are gulps of water that make you more thirsty.

Salmon said yes! That was a little under a year ago and it's all still too close to view. In time, I might be able to look back and see how it fits into the pattern, but for now all I can say is the book was published and launched in Listowel in May 2008. Since then, I have done a few readings and with each one have settled my feet deeper into the book, so to speak, when I get up to read. But there is also an urge to get on with the next one. Many times, I want to crumple up what I've written and throw it in the bin (except you can't do that to a computer screen, and deleting can't be retrieved and smoothed out). But there is an eyeless, mouthless creature inside me that needs me to see and speak for it. It butts its head against the inside of my chest and pushes me on.

Each publication of a poem or book gives this creature the chance to be examined by my inner eye, which checks its state of health, whether its cramped or has room to breathe. If I neglect it, we both suffer! This is the creature that wants to be born but never can be. The best I can do for it is make space — and keep making space — for it to receive the world through me and then clear the world back out, through poetry.

Recommended Reading:

An Duanaire 1600-1900: Poems of the Dispossessed
(Sean O Tuama and Thomas Kinsella. Dolmen Press)

Recommended Website:

Poetry International Web — www.poetryinternationalweb.org

Caroline Lynch was born in 1976 and grew up in Cork. She studied Law in UCC, taking part in student theatre productions. While in college, she was the inaugural winner of the Sean Dunne poetry competition. On completing her degree she studied acting and worked as a professional actor for a number of years. In 2001 she was short listed for the Seacat/Poetry Ireland award. She was granted an Arts Council Professional Development Award and obtained an MA in Writing from NUI, Galway. Her poems have appeared in *Poetry Ireland Review*, in an anthology of new writing — *The Incredible Hides in Every House* edited by Nuala Ní Dhomhnaill — and in *Writers Seeking Lovers*, a collection from the MA in Writing. She won the Listowel Writers' Week poetry collection competition in 2007. The winning poems — entitled *Lost in the Gaeltacht* — were published by Salmon in 2008. She lives in Galway and is working on her next collection.

Celia de Fréine

(Dublin, Ireland)

Writing poetry in Irish

Why write poetry and, if so, why write it in a minority language? There are no real answers to these questions, but here are a few suggestions that shed some light on the matter. Other essays in this book will have covered the basics of how to write poetry. I'll deal with the peculiarities involved in writing it in Irish.

There are many reasons why people write in Irish. Some are native speakers, in which case they automatically write in their first language. But for most of us, this isn't the case: we choose to write in a language which few can speak and fewer can read. Some may have moved to a *Gaeltacht* (Irish speaking) area; others may be inspired by their love for the language or be politically or culturally motivated. Whatever your own reason might be for writing in Irish, it's valid.

Where writing in Irish is concerned, the debate of native versus non-native speaker continues apace. In the early part of the twentieth century some critics felt that as long the language was of a high standard, it didn't matter about style, theme or content. A century later I feel that this attitude still prevails in some quarters and that the Irish written by a native speaker is favoured above that of the non-native. There is a vast army of urban speakers of Irish on this island; we live in a multi-lingual, multi-racial society. Surely it's time to recognise all Irish dialects, whether urban or rural. The Irish language is the first language of this state; it belongs to everyone in this country.

If you want to write in Irish and are worried that your Irish may not be of a high enough standard, set about improving it. There is nothing more tedious than listening to an English-language poet drone on about how they would love to write in Irish but can't because their native language has been stolen from them by an imperial power. If this is the case, why not reclaim it – it's there for the taking. There are Irish language refresher courses and conversation classes in city, town and village, not to mention books aplenty, and a radio and television station devoted to it.

My reasons for writing in Irish are threefold: when I heard my first words of Irish in school, I hungered for more; my journey was no more difficult than that of anyone else living in the *Galltacht* (the English-speaking part of Ireland); I pursued the language down scholastic labyrinths and along *Gaeltacht* boreens until I became fluent. The second and third reasons concern my style of writing. When Samuel Beckett was asked why he wrote his plays in French, he replied that it was only through writing in a language other than his native one that he could achieve the sparsity of words needed for his work. This approach can be an advantage, especially in poetry where it's essential to be succinct: when writing in Irish I go straight to the heart of the matter. Lastly, I find that it is through Irish that I can successfully mine the stuff of my imagination; Irish is better suited to my surreal style. You could argue that I haven't chosen Irish, Irish has chosen me.

As a large percentage of current Irish language writers belong to the older generation, a major concern for some time has been the dearth of younger voices. Thankfully, a new generation is beginning to find their voice – you can read about them at scribhneoirioga.blogspot.com. But it's important to note that you can begin to write at any time. Those having just taken pen in hand are often referred to as 'new' or 'young' writers. Such terms can be off-putting. People begin to write when they can no longer resist the urge not to, or when they can find the time to do so. For many this can be after they have raised a family, retired from a demanding job or when domestic arrangements allow. Emerging seems to be the best term for describing those who are beginning to grapple with the craft of writing.

Once you've begun to write poems in Irish: what next? My advice is to join a workshop. Poetry workshops are organised regularly, with the support of *Foras na Gaeilge*; further information from feasta@eircom.net. You could also set up your own group. A workshop is a good platform for first presenting your work and feedback can be helpful. However, it sometimes happens that workshop criticism can be ill-informed and can do more harm than good. But sharing your work with others involved in the business makes more sense than sharing it with a granny or spouse who have no experience of critical analysis. Show it to these when it has been polished – they're your readers and supporters. Finally, when you've found your voice, you will know whether your poem works or not but, even then, a workshop can be a useful forum for testing the waters before reading to a wider audience. A peer group will also provide you with friendship and support; it will enable you to exchange information about writing opportunities and competition details.

Study the market: read poetry journals before

submitting your work; check your style of poetry against that favoured by the editor – if s/he likes nature poetry that rhymes and you specialise in free-form urban poetry, don't waste your paper and postage. Poetry journals such as the Poetry Ireland Review, Cyphers, The SHOp accept work in Irish; *An Guth*, *Comhar* and *Feasta* are devoted entirely to Irish language work.

As you become more confident, enter competitions: there is an Irish language category in the Dun Laoghaire Rathdown and Strokestown competitions; *An t-Oireachtas* makes awards to Irish language poetry. When you have completed a collection, submit it to a publisher. The main Irish language poetry publishing houses are *Cló Iar-Chonnachta* and *Coiscéim*; Arlen House is now publishing work in Irish. My first book of poetry *Faoi Chabáistí is Ríonach*a was published by *Cló Iar-Chonnachta*. Their policy, at the time, but which no longer applies, was that all books selected for publication, had to be submitted through a competition, judged by independent judges. Publication depended on how well manuscripts did in that competition. My book received the runner-up prize; my second book *Fiacha Fola* won the competition.

Sometimes it is expected that those who write in Irish should be steeped in Irish myth and lore. Ignore this attitude; in fact, the more eclectic or bizarre your terms of reference, the greater the energy you will bring to your work. Welcome whichever muse arrives on your doorstep; embrace whichever tradition you like.

The more you develop as a poet the more you will find that there are many advantages to writing in Irish. Some of these lie within initiatives organised by Ireland Literature Exchange and Literature Across Frontiers who were established to promote work in minority languages. My first book *Faoi Chabáistí is Ríonacha* has been translated into Bulgarian and Romanian, thanks to ILE who financed the translation. As a result of an LAF initiative I have spent a month in Slovenia. A selection of my poems has been translated into Slovenian and broadcast on Slovenia's national radio; in 2007 I read at the Vilenica Festival.

There are also incentives, commissions, and awards, for writers of Irish: *Bord na Leabhar Gaeilge* gives grants to both publishers and authors each time a book in Irish is published. *Bord na Leabhar Gaeilge, An Coiste Téarmaíochta* and *ÁIS* have now all been brought under the umbrella of *Foras na Gaeilge. ÁIS* has the monopoly on the distribution of books in Irish. Distribution is a problem, not least because few shops are willing to stock poetry in Irish. Apart from these, there is *An Siopa Leabhar* in Harcourt Street in Dublin; you can also buy online. Amazon sells books in Irish as do Cló Iar-Chonnachta, who have a sale twice a year (www.cic.ie).

Another challenge regarding writing in Irish is the shortcomings of the language itself: grappling with any language can be a problem but because of the suppression of Irish, there are many gaps in its development; had it developed naturally, it would probably have become much simpler than it is now, shedding certain difficult grammatical structures, as other European languages have done. Few people speak Irish that is accurate: many speak Irish that is littered with Béarlachas – phrases translated using an English syntax; others import words from English. Writing Irish as it is spoken is fine if you're writing a play or a film but, when it comes to poetry, it is expected that the language be as accurate as possible.

My advice is to keep it simple: avoid long sentences and difficult structures; for example, a dash can be a useful way of eliminating the fall-out from cumbersome grammar; double check everything before sending it out. The English-Irish dictionary *De Bhaldraithe* and the Irish-

English one Ó *Dónaill* are both out of date, both having been published over forty years ago. Fortunately, *An Coiste Téarmaíochta* meet regularly to decide on the Irish version of words that have since come on stream; these can be found at: www.acmhainn.ie. The Ó *Dónaill* dictionary has been issued on CD ROM (Win*Gléacht*) and is an essential aid when it comes to checking that *tuiseal ginideach* or *modh coinníollach*.

Remember to read the work of other poets and to attend readings (information from: www.writerscentre.ie, www.poetryireland.ie, www.gaelport.com). Sales of poetry books are small and smaller still in Irish. If you choose to write poetry in Irish, you won't make a fortune; it will probably be a long uphill struggle but a rewarding one. *Go n-éirí leat.*

Recommended Reading:

An Duanaire 1600 – 1900: Poems of the Dispossessed
    edited by Seán Ó Tuama with verse translations
    by Thomas Kinsella (The Dolmen Press)

The Penguin Book of the Sonnet edited by Phillis Levin
    (Penguin Books)

Celia de Fréine is a poet, playwright and screenwriter who writes in Irish and English. She has published three collections of poetry: *Faoi Chabáistí is Ríonacha* (2001) and *Fiacha Fola* (2004) both published by Cló Iar-Chonnachta, and *Scarecrows at Newtownards* (2005) published by Scotus Press. Her poetry has won several awards, including the Patrick Kavanagh Award and Gradam Litríochta Chló Iar-Chonnachta. *Mná Dána*, a collection of plays, each of which has won the Oireachtas na Gaeilge award for best play, is due from Arlen House. See: www.celiadefreine.com

Nessa O'Mahony

(Dublin, Ireland)

Finding the Story

Writing poetry is not for the faint-hearted. The act of trying to capture and distil the essence of something – a moment, a sensation, an experience – and using the best words in the best order, as Coleridge once said, in order to express that essence, can turn a sane woman mad. But we try, some of us, off and on, convinced in our own ways that we are scratching our names on glass, rather than writing them on water (that was from Keats, another unfortunate role model for the nascent poet). But if writing poetry is not for the faint of heart, what then of publishing the stuff? Can there be anything more foolhardy, more vainglorious than seeking an outlet for our private musings. And if we do so, are we ready for the repercussions of our rashness?

The reasons people turn to poetry are myriad and beyond categorisation. The experiences people have when trying to publish their poetry are easier to catalogue; we all tend to share similar sensations of elation and depression, satisfaction and annoyance when our poetry is accepted or rejected, deemed to be of sufficient standard or to have failed the quality test. The trick, and it is indeed a trick, is to remain convinced that there were good reasons why we wrote what we wrote and, while we can always learn from the constructive feedback of enlightened readers, we can never let the judgement of others decide our fate as writers. This is true when having your work rejected, but even truer when, having had your work published, you come to have it reviewed.

I once took a poetry course with a woman who had published a poetry pamphlet over twenty years previously and who had stopped writing entirely because of a negative review that had appeared in her local newspaper. She signed up for the course because she hoped it would get her writing again, and give her back the confidence those two decades had not managed to replace. I would love to tell you that the course was the making of this woman; that she gradually grew in self-belief and approached her writing with renewed vigour. Alas, the scars inflicted by that early review proved too deep to be healed; indeed, the very act of taking the course, which involved a certain amount of energetic workshopping from fellow-students and tutors, convinced her that her work was inadequate. Perhaps she was her own severest critic, but perhaps, too, she had an over-reliance on the reliability of other people's judgements.

Stubborn self-belief (though not mis-placed arrogance) is a vital quality in the poet, as is the ability to remember why we turned to poetry in the first place. It wasn't about affirmation from the outside world, but because through poetry we had found a way to describe our world that no other form of expression could achieve. That, of course, is a very subjective stance. But I'd also argue that objectivity, the ability to step outside one's own pre-occupations and see one's work as an outsider might see it, is an equally vital quality. There is frequently a narrative, a dynamic unseen by the writers themselves as they are writing individual poems, but that becomes clear when those poems are assembled into a body of work. I learned a valuable lesson in this from the editor who worked with me on my first poetry collection.

Just like many new writers, I had gathered together a group of poems that I felt were my strongest and therefore suitable to be collected in book-form. It didn't strike me that the very act of assembling those poems together created a new entity, a book that told its own story, though it was one I didn't realise that I was telling. Because he was outside the creative process of making the poems and therefore objective, my editor could see the narrative arc and, more importantly, the telling gaps where I had been leading up to something and then had side-stepped it: evaded some truth that I hadn't been prepared to face. While this mightn't have been obvious reading individual poems, it became glaringly obvious when the poems were gathered together. My choice was stark: either I faced my demons and wrote poems that specifically bridged those gaps, or else conceded that I wasn't yet ready to publish a collection. I chose the former course, and although those new poems were among the most difficult I've ever had to write, I was incredibly glad afterwards that I had been brave enough to write about what I'd previously considered impossible. I was also very grateful to that editor who'd had the perspective to see the truths buried in the poems and encouraged me to unearth them.

After that experience, I became conscious of the hidden narrative in my poetry, which may be one of the reasons I veered towards more explicitly narrative poems in my own work. But not every poet wants to tell a story and is simply happy to express the lyric impulse in as fresh and distinct a way possible. And yet I fervently believe that even here there is an embedded narrative, and that narrative is visible in the way they see certain images, in the mindset with which they greet a particular landscape, which reveals itself when poems are collected and arranged carefully. The strongest collections have been attuned to the secret patterns of the poems, which is why they are the most satisfying to read.

Mention of reading other poets brings me back to the most compelling reason why most of us strive to publish. We all have 'significant others' in the poetry world, writers whose words first captured us and made us want to emulate them. Being part of a dialogue with writers who have gone before, who are writing along side us and who will come after us, fulfils one of our deepest needs as poets. Our names may be 'writ on water' but our words might echo in the chorus.

Recommended Reading:

Richard Hugo, *The Triggering Town*

Recommended Website:

The Guardian Online Poem of the Week:
www.guardian.co.uk/books/booksblog

Nessa O'Mahony was born in Dublin and lives there. She has published two collections of poetry; her verse novel, *In Sight of Home*, is being published by Salmon in 2009 and a third collection will be published by bluechrome, also in 2009. She was awarded a literature bursary by The Arts Council in 2004 and by South Dublin County Council in 2007. She is currently artist in residence at the John Hume Institute for Global Irish Studies at University College Dublin.

Publishing it

Joseph Woods

(Dublin, Ireland)

So You Want to Emerge?

Poetry Ireland is the national organisation for poetry and poets in Ireland. An essential part of its remit is supporting, encouraging, and assisting emerging poets in their development. We assist emerging poets in the following ways:

POETRY IRELAND INTRODUCTIONS SERIES
This is an annual series and is open to emerging poets born or residing in Ireland. It is aimed at poets with a track record of publishing individual poems and who are working toward a first collection or book of poetry. Applications consisting of 10 poems and a literary CV are independently judged by an established poet and each year, up to 15 poets are selected. The selected poets are given a free one-day master class and a paid reading by Poetry Ireland which is seen an endorsement by the organisation.

CRITICAL ASSESSMENT & PUBLICATIONS

An emerging poet can submit up to 15 pages of poetry, which is then critically evaluated, independently and anonymously, by an established poet and a report is presented. This service, like the *Introductions* series, is not for complete beginners. A small fee is charged and passed on directly to the poet who does the evaluation.

Emerging poets sometimes get through the difficult process of selection by the editor and are published in the *Poetry Ireland Review*, often alongside established and international poets. Publication in *Poetry Ireland Review* is seen as an important stage in the career of any emerging poet.

Through our website, www.poetryireland.ie, and newsletter, *Poetry Ireland News*, we offer advice to poets at all stages of their careers. The website hosts information on everything from lists of journals and publishers to writers' groups. It includes a lively forum for writers. In addition, it includes practical advice on how to make a submission to a poetry journal and how to prepare a first collection. You'll also find a very sensible essay, *Advice to a Poet*, by Maurice Harmon. The newsletter provides news of readings and events, alongside opportunities available for poets.

Through these initiatives we aim to discover and foster new talent, and give advice or provide useful assistance to new or emerging poets. The success of these schemes is measured by the fact that most poets who are now established in Ireland have either participated in some of the schemes outlined above or used one of these services at some stage over the years.

Despite the information we disseminate, through our website and newsletter on the steps involved in publishing poetry, we still get lots of calls to the office from people who have written not a poem, or a handful of poems, but an entire book of poems! This book is usually written in isolation, but sustained by praise from the caller's friends. By the time they contact us, never having had a poem published, they eagerly want a book published – immediately if possible. I often respond by saying you wouldn't expect a record producer to produce a CD of your songs if they've never heard a song of yours on the radio. The same rule almost always applies to poetry publishers. It's a peculiar fact that some people write entire books of poems, without being much interested in contemporary poetry, or indeed, poetry itself.

The following are a few observations, which I hope are useful to emerging poets. If you are starting out as a writer of poetry the obvious place to begin, is by *reading poetry, reading lots of it and reading widely*. Why? If you don't read lots of contemporary poetry you're liable to be constantly re-inventing the wheel when you write a poem; and the likelihood is the theme/subject has been done before and done better. Reading informs us as to what's out there and directs us to places where we can learn.

It is easier to write a mediocre poem than to understand a good one.
MONTAIGNE

There's a surprising agreement and similarity between poets in what qualifies as subject matter for a poem, but there's a huge difference when it comes to individual treatment of that material. By reading, we find explanations for our own tastes and we develop a capacity to make judgements and develop a critical discernment of our own.

READINGS

If you are living in a town or city where there are regular poetry readings, you have a gift on your doorstep. Attending poetry readings develops your critical skills and you can quickly discern and focus on what works for you, and what doesn't. You'll also develop your own ideas as to how your own work should be delivered. Unfortunately, in my experience, emerging poets aren't great attenders of poetry readings, expect where it's an open mic and they have the opportunity to read themselves. Learning isn't all about participation. Even from a poor poetry reading you can walk away enriched; you might have heard a great idea for a poem that was poorly executed. A poor reading might deliver an original idea, or even a daydream, you can use. Alternatively, you can leave a good reading with a sense of being invigorated, affirmed in your belief that poetry is a course you have set yourself upon.

Perhaps most importantly of all, by attending readings or organising them, you are becoming engaged and involved in literary culture and the wider literary community. Emerging poets are often disengaged from this community, perhaps in the belief that the isolation of the "poet in the garret" is best. By participating, you might even get to know a poetry publisher and you can offer to help them unload a box of books from their car!

CREATIVE WRITING COURSES/WORKSHOPS

These can be an excellent way to kick-start the process of learning about poetry; stretching yourself as a poet, and reader. No one can teach you how to write, but you can learn about technique and the possible pitfalls. This spares you going down certain cul de sacs. It's also worth remembering that while the teaching of creative writing is considered novel and new in some countries, including

Ireland, it's been long established in America. Of course you can now pursue an MA or MPhil in Creative Writing in most Irish universities, but these courses are for people with a history of publication. If you are taking an evening class, make sure you do your own research, and that the teacher has a good track record and/or is a poet you respect. If you don't know their work, find it and read it and see if it appeals to you. If the work doesn't appeal, you might need to find another teacher or course.

WRITERS' GROUPS

Use the same caution in joining a writers group as you would in joining an evening course, research what kind of track record they have of publication. Also, see how weighted the group is toward poetry, if you're the only poet among prose writers you might not get a fair hearing. A positive aspect of writers' groups that meet regularly is that they ensure participants are producing new work, and writing frequently. A possible drawback is that the group, or the criticism, can get a bit tired. Sometimes the group can be dominated by strong, and not necessarily talented, personalities. Both Creative Writing Courses and Writers' Groups should be used as training grounds to develop and hone your skills as a poet; they should be a stage on the journey; not the final destination.

PUBLICATION

There is nothing more insignificant in the world of letters than the publication of a first collection of poems.
Herman Melville

Most emerging poets are in a rush to have a book published. A few poets are proud of their first collections but for many, the haste in having a first book published might well be the source of embarrassment. The way to avoid this is to test the poems first, get as many of them published in journals, magazine and newspapers as possible. Seeing a poem in print often acts as a final proof and you might see something you'd like to change or revise when the poem appears in book form, hence in the acknowledgements of many books of poems you read 'some of these poems or versions of them…'

If you don't like the poetry published in a particular journal, don't submit your poems, as the chances are the editor will not like your work either! Certain poems have certain homes. By familiarising yourself with various journals you can build some idea as to what these editors like to publish. This allows you to be more discerning about the kind of poems you send them. Remember, also, that just because an editor rejects your poem it doesn't mean the poem is a poor one. Take a second look at it, revise it if necessary, and send it somewhere else.

COMPETITIONS

Winning a major competition can help get your work noticed, not just by your peers, but also by a publisher; especially if the competition is widely known and regarded. Unfortunately many competitions are not regarded or known. Like Workshops and Writers' Groups, the same rule applies; if you haven't heard of the judge/poet do you want to be judged by them? It's also worth remembering that while many competitions will advertise widely for entries, once the competition is over and awarded, they invariably won't bother to send out a press release or publicise the winners or runners-up. Lastly, there is a recognised 'competition-winning poem', one that appeals to a committee of judges, that uses the full canvas of the standard limit of 40 lines, has a start, middle and end, and tells a story. This kind of poem might not be the one that will inspire a publisher to pay more attention to your work. An alternative to the one poem competition can be the pamphlet or manuscript competition in which the winners have the bonus of being published.

Lastly if you feel, in the full light of your critical ability, that you have something to say and that you have an original way to say it, persist and persist. Don't get disillusioned. Remember poetry can be a lifetime commitment and while some poets are early burners, others are late starters and are in it for the long haul. Some excellent collections of poetry have been published in recent years by people who have waited until retirement to publish.

Recommended Reading:

Memories of the Unknown, Rutger Kopland (The Harvill Press, London 2001. English translations by James Brockway)

New Directions Anthology of Classical Chinese Poetry, edited by Eliot Weinberger, (Anvil Press, London 2007)

Joseph Woods is a poet and Director of Poetry Ireland. Born in 1966 he studied science and also holds an MA in Creative Writing. Widely travelled, he has lived in Japan and travelled extensively in Asia and Latin America. A winner of the Patrick Kavanagh Award, his two collections, *Sailing to Hokkaido* (2001) and *Bearings* (2005) are both published by the Worple Press, UK. In 2007 he co edited *Our Shared Japan* (Dedalus Press), an anthology of contemporary Irish poetry concerning Japan.

Stephanie McKenzie

(Newfoundland, Canada)

Some Reflections on Writing Poetry and Publishing in Canada

I am a poet, editor, professor, critic, and ex-publisher. To date, I have one collection, *Cutting My Mother's Hair* (Salmon 2006), and another forthcoming, *Grace Must Wander* (Salmon 2009). I have co-edited three large anthologies of "international" poetry (*The Backyards of Heaven: An Anthology of Contemporary Poetry from Ireland and Newfoundland & Labrador; However Blow the Winds: An Anthology of Poetry and Song from Newfoundland & Labrador, and Ireland* and *The Echoing Years: An Anthology of Poetry from Canada & Ireland*). I co-published (with my company, Scop Productions Inc.) the first two with The School of Humanities, Waterford Institute of Technology (Waterford, Ireland). I am an Assistant Professor in the English Department at Sir Wilfred Grenfell College, Memorial University, in the province of Newfoundland and Labrador. With a former colleague, Martin Ware, I co-edited the selected poetry of Newfoundland's well-loved people's poet, Al Pittman: *An Island in the Sky: Selected Poetry of Al Pittman* (2003). Recently, I also published a book of literary criticism with the University of Toronto Press, *Before the Country: Native Renaissance, Canadian Mythology* (2007). Despite the diverse nature of these publications and experience, I tend to trace my output and faith in poetry and publishing to what is in many ways my favourite publication, *Humber Mouths: Young Voices from the West Coast of Newfoundland and Labrador.*

Humber Mouths (the first edition) was published in the early spring of 2002 and was the end result of a writing group that I ran and oversaw during the academic year. In 1998, when I first moved from Toronto to Corner Brook, Newfoundland, to teach at Sir Wilfred Grenfell College, I was fortunate to meet Al Pittman and to become good friends with him. Al was no longer teaching in the English department at the college (where he had taught for over twenty years), but he still maintained his position as writer-in-residence. We inevitably decided to begin running writing groups for students and community members. We were both clear from the start that these groups would not be institutionalized but would be held on a weekly basis in various homes. Between 1998 and 2001 we must have run about three to four groups, and in 1999, the group culminated with a modest reading at Casual Jack's Roadhouse (a local pub which has since closed, but which fostered and provided a space for arts-related activities for a number of years). The students decided to call this reading The April Rabbit. This name was chosen because students wanted to walk in the shoes, so to speak, of The March Hare, Atlantic Canada's largest literary festival that has now been in operation for over twenty years and whose birthplace is Corner Brook, Newfoundland.

This April will be the tenth annual April Rabbit, and it has grown from a small event to a very large gathering where sometimes hundreds of people show up to listen to emerging talent on the West coast of Newfoundland. When Al Pittman passed away in 2001, I continued to run a writing group, and when the semester ended (and we were ready for another April Rabbit), it seemed fitting to produce something in Al's honour. He was a senior poet who devoted his time, without any ego or pretense, to sharing his expertise with us. He was very much the spirit behind the creation of The April Rabbit. In the past, students/community writers had sometimes photocopied their work and circulated their poetry on sheets. Then, one member of the writing group suggested we put out a fancier version of the group's work. We were all getting excited, and I suggested that instead of just a fancy photocopy we could perhaps produce something that looked like a book. Now even more excited, someone said to me, "What's the difference between something that looks like a book and a book"? That was it. I thought of a company name – Scop Productions – found a local printer, garnered a small amount of funding at the college and began compiling the first edition of *Humber Mouths*.

I had not yet incorporated Scop as a business (that came later), but, together, the group and I, with about $600, produced several hundred copies of *Humber Mouths*. With this same funding we decided that we'd like to launch the book not only in Corner Brook but also St. John's, the capital of Newfoundland and Labrador, which is about eight hours away by car. We did a bit of fundraising, but had to cut corners. We didn't have enough money for a colour cover or for varnish, and we couldn't stay the full weekend in St. John's. But we were flying high. We packed ourselves into a van and headed off. Several hours into the drive, someone squealed from the back, "Oh my god, my fingers!" Then someone else. Then we all looked at our hands and fingers. They were all stained black. Varnish was not the wisest cut to make when it came to budget considerations!

That night, reading at The Ship Inn, the readers (I was

the organizer and overseer and did not read or include my poetry in the book) were fabulous. And we made municipal, provincial and national news. The poets felt like rock stars, and deservedly so. We had had rehearsals, and we had been trained how to read professionally from microphones. And we had books to sell. We cut the price of the collection from $10 to $5 to ensure more sales and better distribution, and, then, we collectively panicked as the first potential customer began circling the table in a crisp white dress. "Keep her away," one of the writers hissed at me. "Whatever happens, do not sell her a book!" We were floating on nerves and elation, and somehow we managed to avoid staining people's clothes. We spent the night recovering from the excitement and the next day reading the newspaper and listening to the news.

That was almost seven years ago. Since then I incorporated my publishing house, put out the second edition of *Humber Mouths* (in colour and laminated), launched *Humber Mouths* in Ireland and engaged in international publishing endeavors. I have also been fortunate to have secured an Irish publisher for my own poetry. Unfortunately I had to dissolve my own company for financial reasons.

However, despite all the other activities I have engaged in, I still think back to *Humber Mouths* and its Newfoundland launches and realize what I have learned as a poet and publisher.

Disseminating ideas and poetry is a brave act , and an act which fosters hope and confidence. A significant number of writers from that writing group have gone on to arts-related professions, and though there may be a number of reasons for this fact, *Humber Mouths* (the launches and publication) is an important record of their achievements. Publishing is gutsy, and I applaud anyone who can stick with the profession and work towards circulating poetry and ideas. It is an incredibly difficult thing to do here in Newfoundland, the only province in Canada not to have provincial support for publishing houses! It is also a difficult thing to do in Canada. There are two main funding bodies for Canadian publishers: Canadian Heritage and The Canada Council. To access support from the former, "At the time of application, the applicant must have completed at least 36 months of operation as a book publisher". To get Canada Council funds under the Emerging Publisher Grants, "Publishing houses [must] have published a minimum of four and a maximum of 15 eligible titles ... that demonstrate the potential to play an active role in the development of Canadian literature". These are difficult guidelines to meet. After all, how does one publish the necessary titles to get funding, and how does a company stay in business three years as a publisher without funding?

Whatever else, I learned to keep writing, to keep sending material out to journals and presses and to keep supporting other writers – especially emerging writers who have not had much experience or the thrill of getting published. Today, I publish my poetry in Canadian journals (recently with *The Malahat Review* and *The Antigonish Review*), and I attempt to be consistently working on a new collection of verse. I still have the desire to publish the work of others, and to promote literary talent. Poetry demands to be heard and read, and even though there can be hurdles in the way – eight hours of highway, inexperience, financial restrictions – poetry demands a following of people banded together to enable its circulation.

Recommended Reading:

Dionne Brand. *Land to Light On.*
Toronto: McClelland & Stewart, 1997.

Armand Garnet Ruffo. *Grey Owl: The Mystery of Archie Belaney.*
Regina: Coteau Books, 1996.

The Making of a Poem: A Norton Anthology of Poetic Forms.
Ed. Mark Strand and Eavan Boland. NY: W.W. Norton, 2000.

Stephanie McKenzie is is a poet, editor and publisher. She holds a Ph.D. in English literature from the University of Toronto where she specialized in Aboriginal literature in Canada. McKenzie is president and founder of Scop Productions Inc., a west coast Newfoundland publishing house and production company. She is co-editor and co-publisher of *However Blow the Winds: An Anthology of Poetry and Song from Newfoundland & Labrador and Ireland* (2004) and *The Backyards of Heaven: An Anthology of Contemporary Poetry from Newfoundland & Labrador* (2003) and is publisher and co-editor of *Humber Mouths: Young Voices from the West Coast of Newfoundland & Labrador.* With Martin Ware, McKenzie also co-edited *An Island in the Sky: Selected Poetry of Al Pittman* (Breakwater Books, St. John's, 2003). Her first collection of poetry, *Cutting My Mother's Hair* (with illustrations by Michael Pittman), was published by Salmon in 2006.

Works Cited

Canada. Canada Council. "Book Publishing Support: Emerging Publisher Grants."
August 2008. Jan.15, 2009.
http://www.canadacouncil.ca/grants/writing/
of127227340679531250.htm#4.

Canada. Canadian Heritage. "Eligibility Rules for Publishers."
Dec. 12, 2008. Jan. 15, 2009.
http://www.canadianheritage.gc.ca/pgm/padie-bpidp/
dem-app/atp/atp2008-   eng.cfm#rulespubs_regleseds.

Ennis, John, Randall Maggs and Stephanie McKenzie, eds. *However Blow the Winds: An Anthology of Poetry and Song from Newfoundland & Labrador and Ireland.*

Corner Brook, NL and Waterford, Ireland: Scop Productions Inc. and School of Humanities Publications, Waterford Institute of Technology, 2004.

Ennis, John, Randall Maggs and Stephanie McKenzie, eds. *The Echoing Years: An Anthology of Poetry from Canada & Ireland.* Waterford, Ireland: School of Humanities Publications, Waterford Institute of Technology, 2004.

McKenzie, Stephanie. *Before the Country: Native Renaissance, Canadian Mythology.* Toronto: University of Toronto Press, 2007.

McKenzie, Stephanie. *Cutting My Mother's Hair.* Cliffs of Moher: Salmon Poetry, 2006.

Grace Must Wander. Cliffs of Moher: Samon Poetry, 2009

McKenzie, Stephanie, ed. *Humber Mouths: Young Voices from the West Coast of Newfoundland & Labrador.* Corner Brook, NL: Scop Productions, 2002.

McKenzie, Stephanie and John Ennis, eds. *The Backyards of Heaven: An Anthology of Contemporary Poetry from Ireland and Newfoundland & Labrador.* Corner Brook, NL and Waterford, Ireland: Scop Productions Inc. and School of Humanities Publications, Waterford Institute of Technology, 2003.

McKenzie, Stephanie and Marc Thackray, eds. *Humber Mouths: Young Voices from the West Coast of Newfoundland & Labrador.* 2nd ed. Corner Brook, NL: Scop Productions Inc., 2002.

Ware, Martin and Stephanie McKenzie, eds. *An Island in the Sky: Selected Poetry of Al Pittman.* St. John's, NL: Breakwater, 2003.

Chris Mansell

(New South Wales, Australia)

Dear Poet *

Dear Poet

Thank you for sending me your 500 page manuscript entitled 'The Dark Corners of my Mind'. Although you did not enclose an SSAE I saw that you had an email address. If you would like me to return your ms please send appropriate postage. You'll note in our submission guidelines that we ask to see a couple of poems by email only. Please read the guidelines and feel free to resubmit if you wish.

Best wishes
PP

•

Dear Poet

Yes I do suggest that you buy at least one of our titles and no, I don't think that this is outrageous – for a couple of reasons:

1. You'll know what we do. We only publish chapbooks. You'll see that 500 pages is far too much to submit to us.
2. You can show support for the press that you want to support you.

Best wishes
PP

•

Dear Poet

I note you haven't bought any title of any of our poets. Although the book as an object might be endangered, the bookshop as it is now is *definitely* endangered. This press no longer uses them. Poetry sells at launches, readings and through sites and can ill afford the 60% transport/distribution/booksellers discount so we have decided not to sell to bookshops. We give higher royalties to poets instead.

You can easily get a title through the site, but thank you for sending your poem for us to look at.

Do you have anything more contemporary in style? You will see from the poems on the site that the poems are contemporary, have a strong coherent voice and have something to say. That's what we like.

Best wishes
PP

•

Dear Poet

Actually, no, I did not say that your poems were pointless, weak and incoherent. And yes, I do respect experimentation.

I'm not sure that 'Glum Reflections' is a better collection title than 'The Dark Corners of my Mind' – but this jumping the gun a bit.

Yes, I see that the poems you sent were previously published on a website. This does not necessarily mean that they are 'publishable' by us. Many poetry sites have editors and are part of the poetic discourse – which these days is international as well as national and local. Many sites do not. Poems are written for all sorts of purposes and with all sorts of audiences in mind. Every publisher has their own idea about what they are prepared to invest time, energy and money in.

I'm glad your girlfriend likes your poems.

Best wishes
PP

•

Dear Poet

Thank you for the offer of payment to publish your work. It is appreciated but not what we do. Please read the submission guidelines and the attached 'Notes for Poets' which tells you exactly what this press does and does not do if a chapbook is published by us.

Best wishes
PP

•

Dear Poet

I know other presses publish for payment, but not this one. Read the submission guidelines.

There are 4 ways to publish hardcopy books, basically:
1. Self-publish. Where you're upfront about it. You're responsible for everything. You get all the money, all the heartache, all the glory. You can do this through online stores or through your local printer. International online stores give you a listing often.
2. Vanity publish. Self-publish but pretend that someone else is actually publishing it for you. There are quite a few companies around which will do this. Reviewers will see it.
3. Partnership publish. Many reputable companies are doing this in Australia from UNSW (University of New South Wales) Press to much smaller concerns. This means you pay some money but the press does have some say over what they publish and how it is presented.
4. Standard publishing. You submit the manuscript and the publisher decides whether or not they will publish it and they take the risks and pay you royalties at an agreed rate.

We do number 4. It's the way the press was set up and we're unlikely to change it just for one author. Some do a mixture (especially those that do partnership publishing).

Donations are of course welcome but don't expect publication just because you are generous!

with best wishes
PP

•

Dear Poet
If you think small presses are crap, WHY did you submit
to us and waste my time?

with best wishes
PP

•

Dear Poet

Look, I'm not saying that my judgement is the only
judgement. I'm saying I reserve the right to judge what to
publish with my own press. Attacking me is only going to
be counter-productive don't you think?

For the record, like most small press publishers in this
country, I've worked long and hard for poetry and poets in
this country – including setting up two presses of which
this is the latest. Most small press publishers, though not
all, are practitioners of the form they publish, ie. they are
poets themselves. Some presses rely on state government
or Australia Council grants, but many don't, including this
one. Often the person you are writing to is the person
taking the risk.

with best wishes
PP

•

Dear Poet

Thank you for your apology. I appreciate it.

And thank you for considering our press. Unfortunately,
like most presses publishing poetry in Australia, we reject

more than 95% of what we receive, probably closer to 99.5 (ie for every couple of hundred seen one is selected, – but maybe I'm being too optimistic here). So, in the end, I have to say that we can't offer publication of 'Glum Reflections'.

You can see that mostly this is not personal, although because this is a very small press I prefer to work with poets who are reasonable to work with. I subsidise the press with my time, headspace and energy and so prefer to work with people who are positive and reasonable.

best wishes
PP

•

Dear Poet

I did not fob you off! In most cases I would have not answered the many emails you have sent me – but I could see that you were new and your work had possibilities.

This is what a fob off looks like:

> Thank you for submitting your work, unfortunately it does meet our requirements at this time.

or

> Thank you for submitting your work, unfortunately we receive a large number of manuscripts and cannot publish many of the fine works which are submitted to us.

Polite, professional and meaning: *No. Go away.*

A publisher, however big, has a perfect right to be the one who chooses what they will publish. It is their business. Your business is to write as well and with as much integrity as you can.

If, of course, the publishing industry is not how you would wish it to be, I can only suggest that you get out there, do the numbers and set about changing your particular corner of the industry. Most of the publishing in Australia never gets on the official listing of what is published and what sells. Some people say the unreported, small press, part of the figures is about half in Australia. For poetry, it's probably a great deal more – looking at my shelves, I'd say more than 95% of poetry published in hard copy is by small presses. Maybe 99.5%. Perhaps more.

Once upon a time every home with pretensions to knowledge had a *Britannica* – now, no one does. We rely on a diffuse array of sources online – it's vast, and not (completely) centralised (Google notwithstanding). This is what poetry publishing is like today: vast, decentralised, not relying on large publishers but on many, many small publishers. Get used to it. Learn to thrive.

I sincerely wish you well with your work.

Chris Mansell
PressPress
www.presspress.com.au

* This is not a real correspondence, though it could have been!

Chris Mansell is an Australian poet and publisher, born in Sydney in 1953. She grew up on the Central Coast of New South Wales and in Lae, Papua New Guinea, later studying economics at the University of Sydney. She was active in Sydney in the 1970s and 1980s as an editor and poet and since the 1980s has lived in regional Australia where she continues to write, perform, publish and edit. In 1978 she and Dane Thwaites began *Compass Poetry & Prose* a little magazine which published many of the young Australian poets of the time. She closed the magazine in 1987 and soon after, was a member of the collective (which included David Reiter among others) who founded Five Islands Press. She is now the publisher of PressPress. Although primarily a poet, she has also written a number of plays including *Some Sunny Day*. Always interested in experimentation with form, she now also works in digital media. She founded PressPress, a small independent poetry press in 2002 and directed the Shoalhaven Poetry Festival in 2002, '03 and '05. She was winner of the Queensland Premier's Award for poetry, as well as other prizes, and has been shortlisted for the NSW Premier's Award, and the Banjo Award (Victoria).

Gabriel Fitzmaurice

(Moyvane, County Kerry, Ireland)

Publishing Poetry for Children: My Experience

When I was growing up in the village of Moyvane in north Kerry in the 1950s, we learned a lot of poetry in Irish and English at school. But, if we recited poetry in class, we had our own poems on the street – bawdy verses about teachers, bodily functions, sex and so on. They were our secret hoard. They were as much poetry, though of a different kind, as the high poetry we learned at school. But more – they were ours in an adults-keep-out world that we jealously guarded. Roll on the years. I am now at the other side of the desk, a primary school teacher myself. Over the years, I have grown tired of the poems I have been teaching my pupils. So I decided to write a few of my own. My first attempt was "Charlie MacRory" which my class seemed to enjoy. Here it is:

> Young Charlie MacRory
> Has just come to school,

And he never stops crying:
He's a right little fool.

But Charlie MacRory
Is no fool at all:
He got a sweet from the teacher
When he started to bawl. *

Encouraged by their enthusiasm, I proceeded to write more and more poems for children. (By this time I had already published a couple of collections of poetry for adults). I tested all my poems on the children I was teaching which is a privilege afforded to very few poets. Eventually I had enough poems for a publishable collection. But which Irish publisher would publish poetry for children? Very few publishers were interested in even looking at the manuscript. Eventually Liam Miller of the Dolmen Press, Mountgrath, Port Laoise, Co. Dublin, had a look and expressed an interest in publishing the poems. But, alas, Liam died soon afterwards and, with him, his Dolmen Press. Seamus Cashman of Wolfhound Press, Dublin, thought the collection wasn't quite right for them. So no joy there. In desperation, I approached *The Kerryman*, our local newspaper, as they published books from time to time. They were interested. The book, "The Moving Stair", appeared in 1989. *The Kerryman* insisted that I pay Cathy Callan, the artist who illustrated the book, out of my own pocket. Which I gladly did. *The Kerryman* distributed the book to their newsagents. It flew off the shelves. Eventually my book came to the attention of Denis Courtney of the Setanta Book Club which sold books in primary schools. He purchased the remaining stock from *The Kerryman* and put the book into schools all over Ireland. Once again the response was tremendous. Denis Courtney rang me and asked me if I had more poems – that Poolbeg Press (Dublin) and Faber & Faber, London, England, were interested. I asked him who at Poolbeg was interested (it was the editor) and who at Faber (it was, if I recall correctly, somebody in marketing). Without contacting either publisher, I opted for Poolbeg Press on the grounds that I owed it to my country to publish in Ireland and anyway, I'd rather go with an editor than somebody in marketing. A crucial decision. A foolish one maybe. *Je ne regrette rien.*

Poolbeg Press published an expanded version of "The Moving Stair" with illustrations by Donald Teskey in 1993. From then until I left them in 2004, Poolbeg published seven of my collections for children. For sundry, weighty reasons, I moved to Mercier Press, Cork, in 2005. I had already published three books for adults and a book of translations of Gabriel Rosenstock's poetry in Irish for children with Mercier Press and its Dublin imprint, Marino Books. Mercier Press was more to my liking than Poolbeg who, I felt, had more interest in the bottom line, in sales, than they had in books or literature. They were letting an alarming amount of their children's authors go. So, having sold around twenty-five thousand books for Poolbeg Press, I left them for Mercier Press, a decision I have never regretted. I look forward to a long and fruitful relationship with them. *Ad multos annos!*

What advice would I give to an aspiring poet for children? First of all, be sure of your audience – test your poems on children. They will be your best critics. Don't talk down to children – they'll dismiss you in a flash. Remember that poems by adults about childhood may not be suitable for children. Some poets have made that mistake in attempting to write for children and have failed utterly. Children will know if you're on their side – you can't fool a child. When I write for children, I enter a child's mind; when I write for adults, I get to know my own. Don't underestimate a child's intelligence – children can deal with sophisticated themes, they can deal with the big subjects: if not quite birth, copulation and death, they can think and feel and understand deeply. Many children's poets write funny poems, which is wonderful; but one shouldn't make the mistake of being funny all the time. Children can be very serious and can deal with serious poems.

Finding a publisher is another matter. I was lucky – my local newspaper gave me my break when I couldn't find a mainstream publisher. If you can find a literary agent to promote your work, bully for you! But remember, literary agents aren't always interested in taking on poets, particularly unknown poets. So be prepared to go it alone. Remember – most writers get rejection slips, and not just at the beginning of their careers. SO, don't be put off by that rejection slip. Send out that manuscript. And good luck!

* Charlie McRory: From *The Moving Stair* (Poolbeg Press, 1993)

Recommended Reading:

The Complete Poems of Emily Dickinson (Faber & Faber)

A Child's Garden of Verses. Robert Louis Stephenson (Wordsworth Classics)

Gabriel Fitzmaurice was born, in 1952, in the village of Moyvane, County Kerry where he still lives. Before his recent retirement, he taught in the local primary school, where he later became principal teacher, since 1975. He is author of more than forty books, including collections of poetry in English and Irish as well as several collections of verse for children. He has translated extensively from the Irish and has edited a number of anthologies of poetry in English and Irish. He has published two volumes of essays and collections of songs and ballads. A cassette of his poems, *The Space Between: New and Selected Poems 1984-1992*, is also available. He frequently broadcasts on radio and television on education and the arts.

Noel King

(County Kerry, Ireland)

The Doghouse Story

At Writers' Week, Listowel, Co. Kerry in 2003, it was suggested to me that I might consider editing an anthology of writers who had performed at the Poets' Corner series at Harty's Bar in Tralee, Co. Kerry, which was about to celebrate its 10th anniversary. My first reaction was to groan 'not another one' but I came around to the idea. The anthology, *Heart of Kerry*, with contributions from eighty-five writers, was launched on New Years' Day, 2004, under the imprint, Doghouse. A Board of Directors had been formed and the name came from the chairman who donated an office spare which had previously been converted from greyhound kennels. It was announced on that day that Doghouse was open to receiving individual collections for consideration. Within a short time, by accident rather than design, I found myself running a publishing house, albeit voluntarily and for the love and satisfaction of bringing deserving authors, who wouldn't have a chance in 'mainstream' publishing, into print.

By the end of 2008, Doghouse had published twenty-five titles, without any major public funding except for the odd small grant from the Arts Council of Ireland for individual titles. Each title is chosen from a vast collection of submissions of varying quality. One thing that never ceases to amaze us is the naivety of 'poets' who are out there wishing to be published. We've had a query letter a few months ago that read "I was in France in July and started to write poetry, I've fifty written now and need to get a book out for the Christmas market, because I need the money". The response to something like that is 'keep working at it, get them published in magazines and journals' and if you're really lucky you should have a collection ready for submission in six to eight years. If you are still 'blessed by the Gods' your book should be in print within ten years from now. Poems have to be crafted, a first draft is not the poem. It has to be re-worked and re-worked.

Our aim is to publish poets who have worked hard and deserve to have a collection published at this point in their career. They need to convince us that they have a serious dedication to their work and will be available for interviews, publicity and readings whenever the opportunity occurs. The last thing we want to hear is the next example: "I'm retired from teaching and have been writing poems for years, my friends all tell me it is wonderful. My local *Probus* group say they will host a launch for me. I also enjoy golf and tennis." Always check the guidelines – easier these days as they will usually be on the web site of a publisher, saving you having to send an SAE for paper guidelines. People often still don't accept that one has to build up a track record. They think that their work is so good that is deserves book publication NOW. In our guidelines we state no one has ever won an Olympics without first winning smaller local and national races.

The first thing we look at is not the poetry, it is the covering letter and CV. One needs to be satisfied that this writer has served their time in honing their craft. In many cases the name will be familiar from the small presses, competitions, readings and general poetry world which every aspiring poet needs to become a part of – there are plenty of opportunities around the country at festivals, regular 'open mic' events and *slams* to get the work heard. One will know in the first 30 seconds whether a manuscript is worth passing on to the editorial panel, or returned in the enclosed stamped addressed envelope or put in the recycle bin if there isn't an SAE.

We only publish collections with the 'wow factor'; absolutely, totally, brilliant, compelling work. We receive a lot of work as I've said that is just dross or bland (about 50% of all submissions), then about another 40% is quite good work, competent enough but isn't going to set the world on fire. Of the remaining 10% maybe two or three per cent will end up inside the covers of a Doghouse book.

We try to publish a balance of male and female poets and from varied parts of Ireland. We only publish people who are resident in this country. It is impossible to publish anyone from outside as they need to be available or editing, launching and publicity.

Don't approach Doghouse or any other publisher unless you're willing and accept that you are putting yourself 'out there' on show and open to criticism and review. Yes, folks, we've had an author who refused to have a launch as 'poetry is a private thing' and 'I wouldn't want people outside of the poetry world to know that I write'. That is a disaster for a publisher. Our standard contract is now amended to reflect that a writer is expected to do as much as possible to generate sales.

We print 500 copies of each title, about 70 are given away as review copies to newspapers, journals and magazines, and a number to legal (copyright) deposit libraries. We have to personally deliver stock to shops and other outlets, and it can take years for the remaining books to sell. Most wholesalers and distributors will not touch poetry, except for the "headliner poets" of this country, Seamus Heaney, Paul Durcan, and a handful of others. Amazon.com will only list books which come from distributors. This is a real problem for many small poetry presses; and one that isn't highlighted enough. The Arts Council of Ireland gives funding grants to some literary presses, but has never developed a network for promotion of *poetry books*.

So once a manuscript is accepted, what happens next? As editor I read the work over several times and mark it with suggestions for cutting and improvement, and also will put it in some semblance of order if the poet has not already done so. At their own expense the author will travel to me for a number of editorial sessions. What has to be remembered is this has to be the final draft of the poem that's going into the book and it's the last chance to get it right, regardless of where it has been published before. Often some very good work will not make it into the book because the subject matter or style of poem is already well represented. Once the poet and editor are happy with the final draft, endless proofreading and 'tweaking' needs to be done to get it perfect. The choice of book title, cover illustration, blurbs and such is also a long process. A launch date and venue has to be found and a suitable person to make the launch speech.

Costs are always a huge factor and have to be kept to a bare minimum. The poet's and editor's travel and accommodation expenses are always out of their own pockets. Every cent made goes into a fund towards bringing out the next book. Typically, we will post up to 500 paper invitations, then many thousands of emails. The turn-out at launches is typically less than 1% of the number of invitees. Since we can only continue to publish with sales from previous titles, it is very important to hold as many launches as possible. Bookshop and online sales will trickle in, but it's the launch sales that are important. All of this can take many hundreds of hours over many months for each book.

So how much money can a poet expect to make from their book. With royalties at 10% of 9.00 euro and just over 400 units to sell, the poet can expect to make about 350.00 euro at the end of several years – equivalent of one week's work at your local supermarket checkout. There is no money in poetry, but a writer may be lucky to secure workshops, readings and residencies – teaching others how to get on in the world of poetry.

To see more of Doghouse Books, visit www.doghousebooks.ie

Recommended Websites:

www.photonpress.co.uk
www.anthologiesonline.com

Noel King is an actor, writer and editor, native of and living in Tralee, Co Kerry. His poetry, short stories, articles and reviews have appeared in publications in over thirty countires. His debut collection, *Prophesying the Past* appears from Salmon in 2010. He is editor of Doghouse Books.

Primrose C. Dzenga
(Zimbabwe)

Writing and Publishing: A Zimbabwean Experience

Writers and poets all across the world face the same challenges, on two levels: First, Quality of work. If it is good, good enough for whom? Does it have a market? Does it have room for improvement, and, if so, where and who can render the required service of improving it?

The second challenge is getting published. Do we as writers, from different communities with different demands for different kinds of literature, know our niche/our market for our specific genre of literature?

Quality of work, Assessment, and Networking
The only way that any writing in any form or genre will ever get better is through practice. Practice, practice ,practice and practice. One needs to write often and consistently. Over time one begins to appreciate good and bad work – even if it's one's own.

A fundamental aspect about the quality of work is originality; this comes from finding your voice. Everyone has their own distinct voice, and it is crucial to find it.

What the world needs, and ultimately the publisher is seeking, is a fresh voice. My friend who is an editor and publisher always says, "Publishers are like treasure hunters always looking for the needle in a haystack", so as a writer, trying to be that needle, you need to package your work really well for it to be found.

Now, one of the easiest ways of getting your work assessed for free; getting networked and pointed in the right direction, especially if you are in the developing world, is by joining a writers development group (association). Most developing countries have them, for example in Zimbabwe: Zimbabwe women writers association; Budding writers association of Zimbabwe; and, Global arts. In Zambia: Zambia Women Writers.

Most of these Associations are run as professional literary oriented NGOs (Non governmental organisations) that receive donor funding to publish specific works and offer free writers' workshops and subsidised retreats to their members.

They also have very good libraries with a lot of literature, which their members can access easily. Apart from practicing and writing a lot the only other thing that any writer needs to do is to read a lot, and read widely.

Apart from these associations, aspiring writers also need to find out if the British Council has offices in their country. The British Council constantly offers and conducts artist and community developmental programmes, especially for up and coming writers and artists. It runs talent searches (competitions), workshops, and sometimes even mentorship programmes to promising writers. The Tri-nation Crossing Borders project is a mentorship programme for promising and upcoming writers from Zimbabwe, Zambia and Botswana.

By exposing yourself and your work to these

organisations, you stand a better chance of being discovered and being published. A lot of work is published on a commission basis and the people looking for such work almost always go to these established institutions to look for writers. If you are part of such an association and your work is good enough you will usually get noticed. If you are lucky you get your big break.

Of course you don't have to be a member of these groups to get published. Publishers all over the world are always looking for good work whether or not it comes through a writers' group, a literary agent ,or the writer herself; the point here is that being affiliated/connected to these bodies makes it much easier.

Writing is a very lonely career; often writers are alienated from the world around them, and may become reclusive. This doesn't do much for their chances of networking and being published! Especially hard if you are an up and coming writer. Attending writers' workshops and retreats helps to get you out of your comfort zone; to meet other people, get new ideas and possibly get leads on publishers. Thus gaining exposure for yourself and your work.

Knowing your market, getting published, and using the Internet.

A lot of good work goes unpublished because the writers do not know, or understand, the market for their work. Once you have work that you believe is worthy of being published, it is essential to do a little market research. I know "market research" sounds vulgar to all passionate writers. However, it's the same passion that we try to feed and nurture by being published and bringing our work to the right audience!

The easiest way of doing your market research is finding out the type of work a publisher is seeking. In this regard, specifically for, poetry, the Internet is a very useful place. As a rule of thumb poetry does not make money. Few publishers are willing to publish unknown writers (first collections).

The Internet gives you an opportunity to publish yourself, or to be published, online; to be read instantly and get feedback and/or a general view of the quality of your work.

The Internet contains loads of databases of both online and traditional publishers (Writers' Resources directories). It has information on poetry journals, magazines and competitions, both online and print.

A note, especially to writers in the developing world, where access to the Internet is limited: It is worthwhile to spend at least 30 minutes a day at an Internet café; finding publishers and seeing the type of poetry they publish. Also, reading some online poetry, so that you are become familiar with contemporary work.

It is essential to note that, even if your poetry is good, it will be rejected if you send inappropriate work to the publisher; for example, classic poetry to a contemporary publisher.

It's often said that when editors see good writing they will remark on it. If your work gets comments (or a critique) from a serious editor you can be sure that your work is good (editors are very busy people, bombarded by manuscripts daily) even if she/he rejects your manuscript, getting a good comment shows that it has potential, and you should carry on!

Approaching publishers
Publishers are busy people whose business is to find good literature, package it and present it to the world. Different publishers have different markets and different interests. If you find a publisher who might be interested in your work

find out as much as you can about them before approaching them: what their vision is; what they are trying to achieve and what sort of work they publish.

Once one has identified appropriate publishers, it is important to find out if they accept unsolicited manuscripts. This can be easily done by sending a query by letter, or email. For those publishers who cannot be contacted through email, it is essential that the writer encloses a self addressed envelope (SASE) with enough postage for the response. The response may inform you what the publisher accepts, expects, and does not consider, including such things as font and spacing of manuscripts. Some publishers may give you a waiting period before you can submit your manuscript; this means that you must be patient, and send the manuscript at the designated time. Simply because you are made to wait does not mean you won't be published.

Lastly when approaching publishers one needs to be professional. Don't waste time, stick to the point, and outline what you want. Publishers are not looking for adoring fans, but for good work to publish! Have patience, never give up; some of the best books were rejected many times, but went on to become bestsellers when they did get published. Trust your work!

Recommended Reading:

Jessie Lendennie, *Daughter: A Prose Poem* (Salmon)
Charlotte Bronte, *Jane Eyre*

Primrose Dzenga is a young writer from Zimbabwe whose works have been published on the Internet, in poetry magazines and whose first poetry collection is being published by Salmon Poetry. Her first non-fiction work, *The Unsung Heroine – Auxillia Chimusoro*, a biography, is being published by The Women Writers of Zimbabwe.

J.P. Dancing Bear

(Northern California, USA)

Starting a Poetry Press

It's no big secret that most poetry presses do not make money. One reason is because most poetry presses are created as "non-profits". That's a statement on this literary art as a business. Even the large, for-profit, publishing houses do not make money on poetry, even with low print runs. They can afford to write off the loss, while looking prestigious for publishing poetry.

When I started Dream Horse Press in 1997, making it a non-profit entity was one of the many things I had to consider. I asked around to friends who were running presses. Most of them were non-profit, but they didn't like the extra paperwork and grant applications they constantly had to write. I know myself well enough to know that this was not a good choice for me. Dream Horse Press was never going to be my primary business/occupation. So I needed to come up with a model that would work for me. I decided on a "for profit" model even though I knew I would most likely be spending money, not making it.

In hindsight, looking back now that more than a decade has passed, I know I made mistakes. The main one was that I printed 1500 copies of the first Dream Horse title. It was an insane amount of books and for years I had boxes of that book stacked in a spare room, which eventually I referred to as the warehouse. My second release was 500 copies and still I had plenty of boxes of those books too. Traditional (off-set) printing requires more than just paying a printer; there's handling, shipping and storage. The costs were all upfront, so there was never time to meet any of the costs with actual sales of the title.

Owning a poetry press is not for everyone. If you're thinking of starting a press, you should ask yourself a number of soul-searching questions. Owning a press requires a commitment similar to having a child. Are you going to stick with your press for a long time? Are you willing to spend money and time making sure your press is nurtured and will survive? Publishing is a very time-consuming process which encompasses a variety of tasks: checking email accounts; dealing with book buyers; doing accounts; soliciting and reading manuscripts (figure on about 300 to 500 a year); creating ads; editing; either doing design and layout yourself or supervising these processes; working with printers. As well, some authors can be very difficult and time-consuming! .There are costs, large and small, associated with most of those activities. Will you be undertaking these tasks yourself, delegating them, or sharing them with someone else. These are all serious considerations! If you are planning on splitting or delegating the work, are you willing to step in should that person leave? There's also the work arrangement to decide: Is this a paid position; if not, what is this person getting for all his/her hard work?

As I just alluded to, each book takes quite a large number of hours to produce. You will need software capable of producing a PDF file (standard for presses). And you should also consider your printing solutions before you start. So if you are going to use a traditional printer, you'll need to shop around and find the best price for production; crucial questions include the turnaround time, and what your own input will be. It's a good idea to look at customer reviews. You'll also need to consider a distributor and go through the process of what is required to establish a business relationship. If you chose a Print-on-Demand (POD) solution, then you'll want to do the same legwork and determine needs and costs.

After you've covered the basics on costs and printing, it will be time to pick your first project. My advice on your first title would be to make it someone whose work you truly love and/or admire. Then you need to contact that author. I recommend steering clear of friends. There's very old and sage advice about working with friends, and how you shouldn't do it! You will find that you develop a professional friendship with most of the authors you publish. My second recommendation on which project to start with is to pick an author who knows and understands the marketing aspects of small press publishing – so someone with a chapbook (or two or three; or even a full-length book) already published. These authors will have a realistic idea of what happens during the process and are less likely to cause undo tension. It can also be a blessing if they have some direct, hands-on, publishing experience, then they may want to do the layout themselves (with you having final approval). Anything that makes it easier for you is good for your first project.

Other things to consider are whether you plan to self-publish. You should know what you intend to do about this when you start. There's still a stigma associated with it, regardless of how many articles I've seen proclaiming otherwise. I'm not making a judgment here, but I am warning you that others will. You should be prepared for that if it's what you plan to do.

Vanity presses are even more risky for a writer's career. They range in type, but basically the author winds up paying money to a publisher for printing her/his book (invariably, the publisher has no reputation in the literary world). There are some who consider collective presses one or both of the above. Again, these are all things to consider.

You should also consider having a website for your press, with guidelines, and answers to standard, or frequently asked, questions. People won't necessarily write to you to inquire – sometimes they just judge you based on what they can search out about you and your press online.

You should also prepare yourself for the pressures of having to say, "no". Your friends are going to be sending you manuscripts and dropping hints. You are the local press owner, but you may not want to be identified as a local or regional press by publishing local writers. If you are a writer you are now going to be on the other end of the rejection letter, and you need to come to terms with that before you consider your first manuscript. I look at some of my own early manuscripts and I am so glad that they were rejected and NOT published. The editors who were also my friends and had rejected me had done me a huge favor! But it is only with hindsight that I see that.

Overall, the reputation of your press is the most important thing. You want to present good poetry and be known for doing so; otherwise it will not be a joy to publish poetry, and since I've already pointed out the lack of profits involved in owning a poetry press, it had better gratify some other aspect of your life. Everything you do should be to make your press more attractive to talented writers – you want those great manuscripts! My advice to press owners starting out is always the same: be reasonably tough; when you gain a reputation for being reasonably tough the good writers want to be published by you.

J. P. Dancing Bear is the author of *Conflicted Light* (SalmonPoetry, 2008), *Gacela of Narcissus City* (Main Street Rag, 2006), *Billy Last Crow* (Turning Point, 2004) and *What Language* (Slipstream, 2002). His poems have been published in *Shenandoah*, *Poetry International*, *New Orleans Review*, *National Poetry Review*, *Knockout*, *Mississippi Review*, *Verse Daily* and many others. He is the editor of the *American Poetry Journal* and the host of "Out of Our Minds" a weekly poetry program on public radio station KKUP. His next book, *Inner Cities of Gulls*, will be published by Salmon Poetry in 2010).

Todd Swift

(London, England)

The Pros and Cons of Promoting Your Poetry Via The Internet

A few years ago the idea of poets using the Internet to promote their poetry seemed ultra-modern; almost eccentric. Now, it is taken for granted by almost all poets under the age of 60 – and many older, as well. Only a few very prim establishment figures are still offline these days!

The main arguments against using the Internet for publishing one's poetry are: A. copyright issues. B. lack of a "concrete" product, ie. a book. C. lack of quality control. Since almost all journalists now entrust their words to the websites of their major journals and news outlets daily this no longer seems so pressing. However, critics of the net's misuses, such as British poet Wendy Cope, do have a point: If your poetry is online its accessibility could encourage plagiarism or misappropriation. Another concern is that the author is unlikely to be paid.

This last point is the most crucial for poets. I think most poets fall into two categories: those who don't usually get paid for their poems (around 95%), and the well-known poets who get paid by newspapers and publishers. Obviously, if you know that you will usually receive a fee, placing your poems online for free is less appealing. In most instances the trade-off is putting your work online for free, while having the intention of reaching readers who may then go on to order your work (pamphlets or books) online from your publisher's website, or Amazon.com.

I feel that copyright concerns can be dealt with as they emerge. Poets can, and should, "Google" themselves every few months to see if there have been any comments or reviews of their work; then if they discover that their work has been misused they can always contact perpetrators, or take other steps to complain. I also feel that online plagiarism is mostly a red herring; once a poet puts their work out in a little magazine, or book, it is also easily photocopied and stolen by anyone low enough to have such motives.

The other objection is that being "published" online isn't the same as print publishing. Many in the literary community would say that being published in a famous long-established magazine, like *Poetry* or *The New Yorker,* is more prestigious than appearing online, but it is also more prestigious than being published in many print journals. However, most new and emerging poets tend to be published in small, unknown, or little-read print magazines with circulation numbers in the dozens, or hundreds at most. In this way, an online credit in a respected poetry magazine (like the one I co-edit, *Nthposition*), can actually be more useful, and certainly brings more readers.

As younger people tend to read more and more online, and less and less on the page, such online journals do have their own valid and varied communities of readers – and how else is one to be quickly read by poets from Mumbai to Budapest to Montreal? Further, there are hundreds of respected online poetry journals with serious editors. They do exert quality control. They have earned respect by having strict standards.

Nonetheless, as poets gain in confidence, and quality, I recommend they stick to a 30-70 rule. Keep 70% of your poetry for the page, and 30% or so online. Remember, one of the disadvantages of placing work online is that it may stay archived there for 7 billion years; this means, in practice, that one's early poems remain to return and embarrass, and it is hard to repress them. I myself have such poems floating around the cyber ether.

So, having faced the major drawbacks of putting work online, let us now briefly consider the main advantages: A. Ubiquity; B. Freedom; C. Publicity. By ubiquity, I mean that, once one has a blog or Facebook page (few poets require dedicated web sites of their own anymore) up and running – and these take five minutes to set up – it is possible to upload poems, and links to one's digital recordings (MP3s or Youtube-ready movies) of performed work, at will. This instant uploading is then potentially shared with everyone in the world who has computer access.

The dangers of this approach are well-known to all those who have lost their jobs or friends due to uploading the wrong stuff! This is a potential danger, yes, but in reality, one is usually read by, at first, a small circle of family, and friends. My blog, *Eyewear*, has, currently, 54 regular readers, and around a thousand readers a week who drop by occasionally. This makes the blog as well-read as most small magazines.

The second advantage is freedom. The poet is free to post poems without seeking permission from any authority. However, it's important to become familiar with the many vanity presses that thrive on the Internet. Some, such as Lulu, can have non-ego uses – producing e-journals and anthologies; but be warned: if you are asked to pay for publication, then you are dealing with a vanity press. Some vanity presses are subtle...they run competitions and respond to submissions with glowing letters. What the poet doesn't know is that the same response goes to everyone, no matter the quality of the work. While the vanity press may not ask for money up-front to publish poems, they will require book purchases or charge fees for an "award ceremony". At some point you will be asked for money. It's hard not to be taken in by flattery, but, if you are a serious poet, being published by a vanity press is not worth the damage to your career. Self-publishing, also flourishing on the Internet, is different from vanity publishing in that the poet has control over how her work is produced and distributed. There are a number writers who self-published their first book(s), and went on to achieve great success.

The third advantage is publicity. Being able to instantly publicize a reading by Irish poets in Chicago from an office in London is a major achievement for poetry and for poetry audiences. We normally think of an art form in terms of its society; in other words a particular geographic area. The Internet is eating away at that assumption; poetry, as it is discovered by more and more readers, will cease to be a niche art form. It's obvious that promotion and publicity worldwide will encourage poetry audiences; people who may not have thought of poetry in a broad, contemporary, context.

Even on a local level, the ease with which publicity is generated online has created and sustained hundreds of poetry organizations, helping them grow their audiences, and bring in new poets.

There are no get-famous-quick fixes with poetry, however. Many new poets have an overwhelming desire to be published, and to be known, as quickly as possible. In reality, reputations are made and solidified over decades of slow, progressive, serious work; through publishing, promoting others, reviewing, and editing. The only authentic way to become a famous poet is to write good poems that deeply move or interest either vast numbers of people, or critics and academics, or all of the above.

Along with the issues involved in "instant celebrity", there are people who write poetry, but don't necessarily contribute to the wider world of poetry. They tend not to be interested in how poems are made or shared, nor the value of actually buying poetry books. They don't realise the only way to get read by others is to read others. This is a sort of poetic golden rule.

Let me give you a few examples. I am the co-founder of Facebook's biggest poetry group – Poetry. It currently has over 4,600 members. However, last time I checked, few of them had commented on any of their peers' poetry. Or take *Nthposition*. We are read by over ten thousand people each month. However, when we published a poetry anthology, *In The Criminal's Cabinet*, and advertised it at our site, asking for readers to support us, it sold only a few hundred copies. The truth is, for many new poets the Internet is currently seen as a place to get things easily, and for free.

What then, is the realistic advantage of having an online profile? I would say the main advantage is in being able to generate some kind of (even modest) name recognition. If you want to get readings, or submit work to other magazines, having your work available via Google will mean you are all the more likely to appear to be a "real" poet. Further, via social networking sites like Myspace and Facebook, you can form groups of like-minded poets. Starting a blog is also advisable.

On the subject of blogs, though, do remember that the main challenge of keeping a blog is, like a pet it needs to be fed constantly. It also has to be about more than yourself (unless your current personal situation is endlessly fascinating, geographically, socio-politically, or otherwise), has to be updated at least once or twice a week, and has to be well written and original to get much engaged notice. Once your blog is up and running for a few months, you will be able to swap links with other bloggers, and generally build up a readership. All of this Internet work takes time, though – time better spent, in some cases, reading poems, or writing your own.

Poets in the 21st century need to understand the pros and cons of using the Internet to establish a sort of virtual identity for themselves, but this cyber-footprint should not be mistaken for the real world, or the more genuine reasons for writing poems. Poems are an engagement with language and life, and take time and care to write and edit. There is no actual quick fix. That being said, for poets who want to reach out, and share their work with others, a whole word awaits you, online.

Recommended Reading:

> *Harmonium,* Wallace Stevens
> *Soldiers Bathing,* F.T. Prince, (Faber and Faber, 1954)
> *Contemporary Poetry: Poets and Poetry since 1990*
>   Ian Brinton (Cambridge University Press, 2009)

Recommended Websites:

> Jacket magazine – www.jacketmagazine.com
> Silliman's Blog – http://ronsilliman.blogspot.com/

Todd Swift was born in Montreal, Quebec, Canada in 1966, and grew up in St-Lambert. He graduated with a BA in English and Creative Writing from Concordia University. In the 1990s he helped develop spoken word in Canada, with his poetry cabarets. His CD-length experimental text-music collaboration with Tom Walsh, *Swifty Lazarus: The Envelope, Please,* was released by Wired On Words in 2002. A graduate of the MA in Creative Writing at UEA, he is core tutor with The Poetry School, and a lecturer in creative writing and English literature at Kingston University. His recent collection of critical essays about Anglo-Quebec poetry, *Language Acts,* co-edited with Jason Camlot, was a finalist for the

2007 Gabrielle Roy Prize. His poems have appeared in the major anthologies *The New Canon* and *Open Field*; and his poem "Gentlemen of Nerve" was selected to appear in The Best Canadian Poetry in English, 2008. He is the editor of many significant international poetry anthologies, including *Poetry Nation*, *Short Fuse*, and *100 Poets Against The War*; and is the poetry editor of *Nthposition*. In 2005, he edited a special section on The Young Canadian Poets for *New American Writing*. He has had five collections of poems published: the first four were published by DC Books in Montreal, Canada; and, the most recent, *Seaway: New & Selected Poems*, was published by Salmon in 2008. As Oxfam Great Britain's first Poet-in-residence, 2004-2008, he ran the influential Oxfam Poetry Series, and edited the best-selling CDs, *Life Lines and Life Lines 2 – Poets for Oxfam*. He currently lives in London, England, with his wife.

Philip Fried

(New York, USA)

The Manhattan Review: Fidelity to an Irrational Impulse

Starting a poetry journal called *The Manhattan Review* in 1980 seemed perfectly sane and logical, a step to the next stone in the brook. Just out of graduate school, I wanted to publicize the work of poets who were friends, connect with new writers, and astonish readers with my critical acumen. I was even willing to pay a few hundred dollars for this privilege. I did not guess that I was stepping off into the unknown, a decades-long journey that would bring me into contact with writers from around the world (one of the most thrilling e-mail messages I have received is "the mag has arrived in Tasmania") and introduce me to the woman who would become my cover editor, and, oh yes, my wife. Although I could not anticipate the sheer volume of mundane correspondence I would have to churn out and the many times I would have to say, with apologies, "no," I was nevertheless wise in my ignorance. This wisdom consisted not in the sanity and logic of my plan, but in my fidelity to an irrational impulse: the primitive joy of hunting down and bringing back new work.

In other words, I tend to seek out poets I admire and solicit work from them. And I am convinced that to a certain extent, other editors do the same. The dominant model for acquiring new work, however, is not that of the pro-active hunter, but that of the passive baleen whale. Just as such whales feed by swimming near the surface of the water with their mouths open, many literary journals rely on what the flow of mail will bring into their open postal boxes. Both methods have their pros and cons, and I have certainly been delighted by unsolicited manuscripts. I once received, quite unexpectedly, translations of poems by the Polish poet Stanislaw Baranczak, a gift that led to an interview with Baranczak and prompted a pursuit of work by other contemporary Polish poets. In fact, this example demonstrates how the surprise submission washing into your mailbox can inspire a joyful hunt for more of the same. As in many other areas of life, the trick is to find the proper balance between chance and intention.

Overall, I would estimate that I receive about 300 or more unsolicited manuscripts a year. While I read all of them with interest, I accept very few, perhaps one or two. Some of these submissions, curiously, display more passion in the cover letter than in the work itself. I remember receiving a letter from a man who claimed to be living in a warehouse in Phoenix. I suppose the whole thing could have been an attention-grabbing hoax, but the descriptions in the cover letter – the bare walls, the vast space, the forays out into the world – still remain with me though the poems themselves have been long forgotten. In that case, it might have been better if the poems had been consolidated into a cover letter and the cover letter submitted as a poem.

In explaining what I look for in a poem, my citing Emily Dickinson's famous and oft-quoted aphorism – "If I feel physically as if the top of my head were taken off, I know *that* is poetry" – would be some indication but no clear help. So let me take another approach. Sometimes, as we sit down to write, it is what we are sure of that defeats us – namely, that we will be writing some well-defined work called a "poem," which will "express" in "free verse" the "thoughts and emotions" of some well-defined entity called a "self." In other words, if you can arrange to be uncertain about some of these verities, you will be off to a good start: Do I even have a unitary self to express? Is free verse the natural birthright of all contemporary poets?

Often, I find that the most exciting poems are those that convince me they have begun before the first line. The remarkable Dutch poet Toon Tellegen, ably translated by Judith Wilkinson, begins one poem as follows:

> My father
> was immense and limitless
>
> it was raining
> and my brothers were horses
> that trotted
> across the vastness of my father –

Reading these words, I feel I have just woken up halfway down the take-off ramp of a ski jump, traveling at about 80 miles per hour. I must have been poised at the edge of the ramp at some point, but since "the top of my head" has been "taken off," I can't remember when I decided to risk my life this way.

As readers of poetry, we should be prepared to take such risks. Our usual defense against the thoughtful emotions and emotion-filled thoughts of poetry is to say, "This is too strange. I don't understand it. Where is it taking me?" The answer is to create, at least for a time, a certainty-free zone like those drug-free zones near schools in the United

States. Trust the strangeness, and trust your own emotional response to the poem.

Speaking of strangeness, I'd like to conclude with a story in the flea vs. behemoth category. In 1994, *The Manhattan Review*, circulation 500, decided to challenge *The New York Times*. "We" (it was I, wearing an institutional mask and sitting at a typewriter) rounded up 350 distinguished poets to petition the *Times* and protest the scant attention given to poetry in the Sunday *Book Review*. The result was what one colleague, a bit sarcastically, called "The Yalta of Poetry," with Joseph Lelyveld, newly appointed executive editor, and several other editors sitting down to discuss poetry coverage with a small group of well-known poets. It had to be a first, and Lelyveld seemed mildly amused in a courtly sort of way. Poetry reviews actually doubled in number for the next six months, before the lack of coverage resumed, possibly due to a change of editorial management in the *Book Review*. The whole episode was strange enough to be a poem. Under the banner of *The Manhattan Review*, poet-negotiators scored a brief-lived cultural victory, and unlike their slightly more famous Yalta counterparts, didn't have to give away Poland.

Recommended Reading:

> *Song of Myself*, 1855 Edition, by Walt Whitman
> *The Complete Poems of Emily Dickinson*

Philip Fried, a New York-based poet and little-magazine editor, has published four books of poetry: *Mutual Trespasses* (1988); *Quantum Genesis* (1997), which A.R. Ammons called "a major new testament"; *Big Men Speaking to Little Men* (Salmon, 2006) which – said Marilyn Hacker – "represents much of what I admire in contemporary American poetry ....";and *Cohort* (Salmon, 2009). Fried also collaborated with his wife, the fine-art photographer Lynn Saville, on a volume combining her nocturnal photographs with poetry from around the world. And he is the founder of *The Manhattan Review*, an international journal that for three decades has published the best in Anglophone poetry and translations.

Simmons B. Buntin

(Arizona, USA)

Publishing Poetry Online:
The experience of Terrain.org

As the editor of the online journal *Terrain.org* (www.terrain.org), I am often asked about the differences between poetry published online and in print. How is the process of submitting different? What about reviewing? Does the quality vary? Is publishing online as legitimate as publishing in print journals?

The simple answer to all of these questions is that the only significant difference is the delivery medium: a computer monitor or handheld device instead of a paper journal or magazine. Good poetry is good no matter where it is published; likewise, good journals are good whether virtual or paper. The same holds true for bad poems and journals – they can be found in print and online, though perhaps not in similar numbers.

For new and little-published writers, the difference between online and print begins by answering the fundamental question: *What is online publishing?* The easy but incorrect answer is that publishing online is the placement of a poem on a website, which can run the gamut from an online journal (what's often referred to as an e-zine) to a blog to a personal website. But the writer should ask: Is the publication of a poem on a personal website or a blog actual publishing? If someone types up a poem and leaves it at a bus stop or the corner grocery, is that actual publishing? The answer in both cases is no. Publishing, whether online or off, requires an editorial process.

Someone reviews and selects the poems, judging them against other submissions and choosing those she or he feels best complete a particular "issue." Issue is an amorphous term, however, because with online venues, there may not be particular issues but rather ongoing publication and overlap among contributions. Still, they key is the critical editor.

Here's how it works at *Terrain.org*, which receives several hundred poetry submissions and generally accepts work from about a dozen poets in each issue. Like many online and print journals, we now accept submissions through an online submission manager (http://sub.terrain.org), which requires submitters to create an account and then submit by uploading the submission on our website. The value for the submitter is that he or she can check the status of a submission, and withdraw it at any time. *Terrain.org* allows (and I heartily endorse) simultaneous submissions, and the ability to easily withdraw a submission is significant. The submission is logged into the system, which also serves as our database for review and communication with the writer. In the case of poetry, I am the sole reviewer, though for larger (generally, college-sponsored) publications, there may be multiple reviewers, and the system facilitates reviewing and commenting on submissions. Once reviewed, the system offers options for notifying the writer – decline, with multiple types of preformatted rejection notes, and accept, with the ability to add individual notes. The system emails notification, but after that, communication is one-to-one between the editor and writer via email.

As online submission systems become the standard, the submission process gains equity. Still, there are a number of print journals that continue to accept poetry only via post, and that's a disadvantage for those publications. It's much easier for a writer to submit online, or via email, than by traditional mail. Generally, response times for online publications are faster, as well. At *Terrain.org*, we try to respond within eight weeks. The submission system has actually lengthened our submission response period because it takes a bit longer to work through the submissions now than it did when we accepted via email. But we no longer lose the occasional submission due to email outages, either!

The delay between acceptance and publication may be shorter with an online journal. *Terrain.org* has a set publication schedule for each theme-based issue (we publish two issues per year). So if we accept a submission early in our review period, there may still be a considerable delay. For those journals that publish more often, or on an ongoing basis, there is often little delay. Print journals, on the other hand, take longer in part because of the print and distribution process.

Submission process aside, online publications soar in the types of poetry and poetry projects they can support. For example, *Terrain.org* now includes audio of the poet reading her or his contribution, something not possible with traditional print journals. Or consider Born Magazine (www.bornmagazine.com), which combines text poetry with an animated movie and voiceover.

The wide variety of online publications means it may be easier to place poetry online, in a specific niche publication. Experimental poetry or visual and interpretive collaborations with poetry may be more amenable to online placement. Like print journals, e-zines often focus on specific geographic locations, political slants, poetry types, and the like. But unlike print, online journals are quick to access and search via the Internet, as well as online resources like NewPages.com and Duotrope.

Finally, poems appearing in online journals usually receive far more exposure than in print journals. A good print journal may have a press run of only 1,000 copies. Even if three other people read each copy (an unlikely scenario, I fear), then perhaps 4,000 people have access to the poem. Online, however, readership is borderless. Anyone with access to the Internet can read the poems, assuming she or he can find the site or Google the author. It's not uncommon for an online journal to have hundreds of thousands of visits per issue. At *Terrain.org*, we average about 200,000 visits per issue. *DIAGRAM* (www.thediagram.com), another intriguing online journal, receives about three times that traffic, the editor tells me. Assuming the issue is archived indefinitely – the standard for *Terrain.org* and most online journals – the poem literally lives forever. It has no shelf expiration date.

But does varied content and accessibility equal legitimacy? No doubt, many still question the quality of work appearing in online journals versus more established print venues such as *Poetry Ireland, The Kenyon Review,* and *Poetry*. In an online survey I conducted in 2005, more than forty percent of respondents felt there was a difference in the quality – that print journals contained a higher quality of poetic work. Yet the respondents also believed that the biggest misconception about poetry appearing online was that it was not as high-quality as print poetry.

My sense is that, more than three years later, online journals as a rule have gained the same legitimacy as print journals – though there is still a diminishing stigma about publishing online versus in print. Many poets still save their "best" work for print journals, and the best-known print journals continue to receive more submissions than online journals. Even so, well-edited online journals like *Terrain.org* are as legitimate as print journals. Indeed, because of their real-time and increasingly interactive nature, they may be more legitimate in our high-tech, wireless world.

What matters, online or off, is finding a venue that's a real match. Whether publishing on stone tablets or the iPhone, writers should get acquainted with the publication in which they hope to publish, then submit their best work.

Recommended Reading:

A.R. Ammons, *The Selected Poems: Expanded Edition*
Richard Hugo, *The Triggering Town: Lectures and Essays
on Poetry and Writing*

Recommended Website:

The Cortland Review: An Online Literary Magazine in RealAudio (it's looking a bit dated now, but was the original to post poetry audio): www.cortlandreview.com

Simmons B. Buntin is the founding editor of *Terrain.org: A Journal of the Built & Natural Environments*. His first book of poetry, *Riverfall*, was published in 2005 by Salmon Poetry. His next collection is due from Salmon in 2010. Simmons has published poetry widely in North America, including *Orion*, *The Manhattan Review*, *Whiskey Island Magazine*, *Isotope*, and several anthologies. He is a recipient of the Colorado Artists Fellowship for Poetry and an Academy of American Poets award, and lives in Tucson, Arizona.

David Gardiner

(New York, USA)

The health and feeding of one species of fox – The Sionnach

The truth is rarely clear and never simple, St. Oscar said. My original goal was to write a straightforward and helpful narrative of my experiences starting up the contemporary American–Irish journal, *An Sionnach*, and my subsequent experiences as Director of Creighton University Press – an experience as basically my own boss. The more I reflected on the past few years with the journal and the press though, the more it looked like a version of Barthes's *Giles Goat-Boy* and perhaps deserved the same treatment. Telling the tale clearly may be of use since the truth is our best fiction.

An Sionnach takes its name from the Irish for fox. I have been corrected on occasion because the journal title is not *madhra rua*. I know that in certain counties this is what a fox is called. A fox is not a red dog. I have had red dogs before. And I've seen foxes every year that I have lived in Ireland since 1989: up on Prospect Hill in Galway City; sneaking around the corner from Grogan's (the fox not me); running along the road between Coleraine and Portrush; and even one summer raising an entire family behind my rooms at Trinity College in the Provost's backyard. The fox is a survivor and lives on every continent in our world. Or did, if you discount that sad story of the Falkland Island fox which left this earth forever in 1876, but that's another essay.

An Sionnach is originally from Omaha, Nebraska and was not born very auspiciously. In fact, more like its foraging city brethren, it was inspired by its wits after nearly being run over altogether. This reflection is offered as both memoir and how-to guide. A sort of confession of the surreal and, hopefully, an inspiration: However half-baked your desire to start a literary publication might seem, if you can get the right things in place, it may just happen.

An Sionnach is not as it was originally conceived. It was to have been another journal altogether. There had been a fledgling journal devoted solely to contemporary Irish writing based at a conservative Southern Baptist university. One morning, an administrator at that university decided to actually read the publication and was horrified to learn that homosexuals apparently existed in Ireland and that his university was supporting the analysis of this noticeable aberration. After a few months of negotiation with the editor of that journal, the operation was ready to move over to the Society of Jesus run Creighton University in Omaha, Nebraska where it would not be in similar danger. Over the course of months, budgets and proposals were forwarded to, and approved by, Vice Presidents, Deans, and Budget Committees. New editorial boards were contacted and the University Press agreed to modestly fund the new initiative.

This is where the how-to comes into play. I was first approached during my second year as an assistant professor, when I was faced with daunting teaching, advising, and committee duties. As most of us, as a student I had been involved in any aspect of publication I could weasel into – from sports columnist on *The Maroon* at the University of Chicago, to literary editor of the college creative writing publication with modest funding and (oh joy of joys) keys for late night meetings in the English Department, to those "underground" publications we would sprinkle around the student union after gaining access to any computer and copy machine we could find on the cheap. Because of earlier experience and tutelage on American journals, I knew that this new journal would be a different undertaking.

A truly international journal requires a responsible editorial board to establish standards, an adequate level of funding to ensure proper delivery of a quality product, and perhaps most importantly and most over-looked, the work-hour support in which to do it. This last required some release from teaching, or other duties, and hopefully staff. At most universities where journals such as *An Sionnach* are produced, labor is bartered for staff on a daily basis. Frankly, it is cheaper from an administrative basis. Not paying a professor to teach a course allows a part-timer to come in at around 1/10 of the regular staff member's salary to teach that course – while still requiring that professor to retain all their remaining duties. This may not be right, and it certainly isn't ethical, but it explains why the bar for learning and internships within literary journals has lowered to the graduate student, and sometimes even undergraduate, level when it comes to not only proof-reading and correspondence, but sometimes even vetting manuscripts. In the case of *An Sionnach*, I was fortunate in drawing together an experienced and energetic editorial board upon whom I've been able to rely since inception. Regarding funding, because of my experience as a director of numerous international programs in the past (and two terms as treasurer for the American Conference of Irish Studies), I was able to provide clear, transparent budgets for the College and University boards involved. It probably helped, too, that I interned for Allan Kornblum at Coffeehouse Press and saw one of the best, most imaginative small presses in the United States function at the same time as I was beginning a dissertation on Liam Miller's Dolmen Press (Ireland).

There's a sheer and naïve joy in that sense of the opportunity – that it might happen and that people might be involved. But I cannot stress enough having the standards, funding, and labor support worked out in detail. These can be envisioned, and there are enough fellow workers out there to go to and ask about it. I'm not old enough to have ever seen a Mickey Rooney movie. But I know that he starred in Boystown. (In fact, that's all I knew about Omaha when I moved there from my native Chicago: Boystown was there.) Upon meeting the Father Flanagan Division of the Ancient Order of Hibernians (Omaha Division), I understand why Father Flanagan was the only Priest ever escorted out of Ireland too....But back to Mickey Rooney: not having seen his movies, I still knew that he had a famous line in which he barks out enthusiastically, "let's put on a show!" That's what it feels like with any literary exercise at times; most especially with a journal. This was the beginning phase.

The importance of this became entirely clear to me the morning that the most recent species of fox was born – the "stairway fox." One lovely morning in March, I awoke and checked my email. Time stamped somewhere between two and three in the morning, during that golden hour after drinks when "friends don't let friends email," a missive arrived from the editor with whom we had been negotiating. It was cc'd to the Dean, VP, myself, and   the

President outlining in great detail an analogy between the loss of a child and the loss of control over a journal; the wrongs that had been done to the literary world; and some other character libels just for fun. I headed straight to my Dean's office – he was the third of seven I have served under in eight years. I have grown adept at re-explaining the wheel, but this was new. Upon arriving, the administrator summarily said, "Well, I guess that's that." "Au contraire," I quickly and snappily answered, "we have everything in place from the budget to the postal permissions to the ISSN number. We even have a new title." The answer: "Oh, very well then." And thus, with me trying to escape into an adjacent stairwell before the sweat on my forehead became visible, a new journal of literature, culture, and the arts was born. It wasn't until I made it to the stairwell that "An Sionnach" occurred to me.

Things like *The Little Review* (founded in 1914 and "making no compromise to the public tastes") don't really exist any more in an American world of shrinking arts budgets. The truth is that there is no money outside of creative writing programs for literary journals and unless you have huge government grants for publications, the chances of success are severely limited. As opposed to the Republic and the North of Ireland where there still remains (limited) Arts Council funding, we can't appeal outside a very narrow range. Subscriptions will not immediately carry a journal and most conferences and organizations look forward to their free copies at events. Thus we are truly weasels fighting in a hole. And it affects every aspect of the arts. That was one of the reasons why, from the moment *An Sionnach* was conceived, it was viewed holistically, from conferences with our outstanding design editor regarding typeset to careful consideration of an international editorial board that incorporated diverse aspects of American-Irish arts, culture, and business and who would not be caught within the cronyism that pervaded certain other areas.

Though published in the United States, *An Sionnach* has consistently commuted intellectually between Ireland, Europe, and the U.S. This is contrary to the vast majority of sister publications in the U.S. which, as stated, are mainly funded by creative writing programs. A typical morning on any U.S. campus will begin with a trove of email calls for submissions from new or established journals to the Directors of their Creative Writing Programs. These will be "refereed" by M.F.A. students, or undergraduate "creative writing majors," keeping a keen eye out for their professor's colleagues' submissions, all clearly marked, as they come in for another round of publications in anticipation for another round of readings. In the business world this is called "networking." In the arts, it used to be called "patronage." But where there is no money to be had and no real advancement of the arts other than an honorarium, a stay in a hotel, a few dinners, and a line on the vita, I'm not sure what this is called. Having seen this for too long, I conferred with the editorial board and decided early on to be a bit Poundian and hard-headed and open *An Sionnach* to a Quixotian task of covering contemporary "literature, culture, and the arts."

We also set our sights differently. Our copy editor sat with me in Boston one evening and asked what my circulation target was. I pointed out matter-of-factly that we couldn't focus on adding up the revenue from individual subscriptions since I saw too many journals stolen off tables at conferences. We do intensely value each individual who does subscribe to the journal; however from the beginning, our strategic plans sought to outsource our sales and distribution in traditional and non-traditional ways. The former was achieved through an agreement with the University of Nebraska Press – the largest University Press between New York and California. This allowed for proper handling of all the business aspects of the journal while simultaneously dispelling the romantic picture of boxes of journals cluttering up an apartment waiting to be personally posted by the editor. The latter goal was achieved by membership within ProjectMuse, the full-text web database out of Johns Hopkins. ProjectMuse grants us access to global libraries at a pro-rated subscription rate, reaching literally millions of readers through an ethically-based scalable economic model that returns some money to both Nebraska Press and the journal to sustain us through means other than traditional subscriptions.

Ultimately, strategic plans and titles thought up on a moment's notice in university stairwells do not account for quality. That is something that all of us – from those underground journals at university all the way up to Salmon Poetry – can't replicate through all the spreadsheets and mission statements in the world. An Sionnach has been blessed with outstanding contributors from the beginning. Because of the focus of our publication, we began a few years ago with a Special Issue on the writings of greatly-missed late James Liddy, one of the most important and least appreciated American-Irish poets. Thanks to the work of our arts editor, Dr. Sighle Bhreathnach-Lynch (Curator of Irish Art at the National Gallery of Ireland), we began with a cover featuring the work of Patrick Collins. That issue earned mention in The Irish Times and over the five years since the writers we have featured have included Brendan Kennelly, Paula Meehan, Gerald Dawe, Seamus Heaney, Van Morrison, Frank McGuinness, Derek Mahon, Medbh McGuckian, Hugo Hamilton, Theo Dorgan, John F. Deane, Pat Boran, Sebastian Barry, Harry Clifton, and Thomas Kilroy. In keeping with the first cover artwork, we've continued to feature visual art from important contemporary Irish artists and have been fortunate to include works from Robert Ballagh, Liam Belton, Sarah Longley, and Nevill Johnson as well as articles on a number of these artists and a memoir from Johnson along with his Dublin photographs. Challenges remain. Like most university presses in the U.S., the University Press that supports the journal is hardly solvent and could pull the plug at any moment. And, as with any journal focusing on strictly contemporary events, there's a certain amount of blood pressure medicine involved in refusing to keep a backlog of submissions so as to guarantee the relevance of the published work. But, it's in a fox's nature to survive.

What does this tell anyone about writing or publishing poetry? Probably not much except it's still a mare's nest based as much upon chance as determination. I hope that it's more of the latter. And my experiences with An Sionnach tell me that it is.

Writer, publisher, and professor, **David Gardiner** lives in New York City. He splits his time between the U.S. where he teaches Irish Studies and his duties at Trinity College Dublin. Since 1989, when he attended University College-Galway, he has commuted between Ireland and the U.S. A published poet and critic, in 2004, he became founding editor of the international journal, *An Sionnach: A Journal of Literature, Culture, and the Arts* (Creighton University Press) and in 2005 he took over directorial duties of Creighton University Press. His doctorate was earned at Loyola University, under the direction of the late Prof. Seán Lucy. Before that, he studied at the University of Chicago, the University of St. Thomas, & Penn State University. He has published numerous books, articles, and poems. Gardiner is currently a visiting scholar at Boston College, New York University, and the University of Ulster.

John M. FitzGerald

(Los Angeles, California, USA)

Small Press Publishing

I am an attorney and the author of two books of poetry. When my first book won an award and was slated for publication, I took two years off and went to work as the Development Director for one of the most up-and-coming small presses in Los Angeles, Red Hen. My job ran the gamut of independent publishing.

At one time or another I wore every hat: from manager, to editor, to events coordinator, but most of all, fundraiser. As Development Director, it was my job to raise the funds for publication. I sought grants from State and Federal governments, corporations and private donors.

Most governments, and indeed, most corporations and private donors, have very specific criteria for the types of projects they will fund. Many corporations are interested in contributing to the local community, one just has to find them. State and municipal governments limit funding to locally based projects.

In Los Angeles, for example, worthy projects may receive assistance at both the city and county levels, through the Los Angeles Cultural Affairs Department, or the County Arts Commission. Of course, resources are limited and competition is fierce.

Many small presses are non-profit organizations. This means that, unlike commercial houses, they do not survive solely on the income produced by their books. They do not, for the most part, publish bestsellers sold in grocery stores or at the airport, through book-of-the-month clubs or chain bookstores. These are books by writers who, while deserving of an audience, are happy to find themselves on the shelves of even local bookstores.

Small presses which publish poetry, literary fiction and non-fiction do so, typically, as labors of love. Often they were founded by one or two individuals who dedicate a great deal of their own time and money bringing deserving, but little-known, literary work to the public. More often than not, most people never learn that these literary gems exist. There are no billboards or television commercials, no signs in the subway or on the sides of buses. There are no appearances on David Letterman or Oprah. No reviews in the *New York Times*. A small press book of poetry that sells a thousand copies in a year is likely to be among the publisher's best sellers.

The thing most poets and authors don't realize about getting their work published is that they must take an aggressive and active role in the process. "Publication" is not mere printing. Any fool could accomplish that. Publication involves making work known to, and accepted by, as wide a readership as possible. It requires a great deal of work on the part of the writer.

Poets who want to be published must realize that they cannot simply write their books and sit back; they must be publicists and marketers. This is true at each level of prominence they achieve. Liken it to the biggest name movie stars you can think of. They don't simply make the movie; they do the rounds to promote it. Think how much more a little-known poet must do to promote a lesser-funded book!

Poets must be the foremost marketers of their own work. They must give readings and do book tours, often without pay. They must know how to sell their own work.

Often, in the case of non-profit publishers, an author will have to be a proactive participant in raising funds for the project. This does not mean self-publishing. But it may mean providing your publisher with lists of those who believe in your work, and who want to see it published, and might make some contribution toward that end. In short, you must cooperate with your publisher to help move the process along. It may mean providing lists of persons who might pre-order your book, so that the budget for the project may be enhanced. As Development Director, the authors who cooperated with me most had their books move to the top of the publication list, simply because the project had a budget already in place. Alternatively, you can wait for the publisher to handle everything, and your book will come out in a couple of years, behind those of all those authors who are helping to make things happen.

Just as no one makes a living as a poet, small press publishers don't do what they do for the money. Many have regular jobs. Many, perhaps most, are writers themselves who must also find time to write. Publishing, to them, is not so much a business as an act of artistic creation. Nevertheless, to remain in existence, they must necessarily attend to business.

In general there is a good atmosphere for poetry in California. The state hosts a good many literary events. Some of the bigger and better known include the Los Angeles Times Book Festival, and The West Hollywood Book Fair. But there are a good many more, from Petaluma to Palm Springs.

Local bookstores and other literary venues are also excellent resources, not only for keeping small press books on their shelves, but for holding readings and helping to promote interest in literary events. Many bookstores have regular reading series. In Los Angeles, the Ruskin Art Club and Beyond Baroque are two mainstays of the poetry scene, hosting readings and workshops. Established local bookstores include Book Soup, Skylight Books, and Village Books, all of which host readings and signings.

Libraries, of course, are always interested in promoting literature. So anyone with a flair for organizing events can usually get a library interested in book appreciation activities.

As mentioned above, the majority of the people never learn that these literary gems exist. After all, the literary community is a relatively small fraction of the overall population. Therefore, it is vital for those who would be part of that community to help keep it alive by buying small press books. Support the community. In the end, we all depend on each another.

Recommended Reading:

77 *Dream Songs* by John Berryman
The Duino Elegies by Rainer Maria Rilke.

John M. FitzGerald is a writer/attorney in Los Angeles. A dual citizen of the United States and Ireland, he attended the University of California at Los Angeles (UCLA) and the University of West Los Angeles School of Law, where he was editor of the *Law Review*. His first book, *Spring Water*, the fictional story of the mental life of a psychotic bottling plant shipping clerk who poisons bottles of water and ships them to Los Angeles stores, was a Turning Point Books prize selection in 2005. *Telling Time by the Shadows*, a book of poems of love and longing, was released in April, 2008 by Turning Point Books, Cincinnati, Ohio. As yet unpublished works include *Primate*, the fictional tale of a sign-language speaking chimp allowed to testify in court, *The Zeroth Law*, a work of poetic literary non-fiction comparing the beliefs of the world's major religions to history, myth and science, and *The Mind*, a series of poems about consciousness and thought. John has worked as Development Director for Red Hen Press, and is currently the Associate Book Editor for Cider Press Review. He lives with his wife, poet and actress Hélène Cardona, in Santa Monica, California.

Janice Fitzpatrick-Simmons

(Ireland)

Every Solid Thing

I have been writing poems since I was ten years old. I wanted to be a poet and that was encouraged by my 4th grade teacher Miss Hollis. She read out-loud Samuel Coleridge's *The Rhyme of The Ancient Mariner* and Robert Frost's *Death of A Hired Man*. I so looked forward to that reading time, and there wasn't a whisper to be heard in the class as she transported us to that magical space where meaning and sound, image and thought, are a living presence. Other teachers inspired and encouraged me "along the enchanted way". But it was The Robert Frost Place (Franconia, New Hampshire) that set me on the way to The Poets' House and creating (with my husband, the late James Simmons) the first Frost-like poetry conferences and eventually the first M.A. in Creative Writing in Ireland. At the Frost Place I met American poets who began to shape my adult mind. William Matthews, Denis Johnson and Sherod Santos were the young writers in residence. They were 4-8 years older than me and full of ideas and advice and good fun. Bill Matthews gave me advice that I have kept close; "you have stories to tell in your poems, so write about what you know." At The Frost Place I met many American poets and sat in on what workshops my job allowed. I can still see Rod standing at The Frost Place kitchen door. I can still hear James Merrill reading from *The Changing Light at Sandover*. During this time I was also visiting Ireland (1978-1986) and met with various Irish poets and artists about my idea to set up an International Poetry Centre based on The Frost Place summer courses.

One of the best things to come out of my Irish visits was an exchange between The Robert Frost Place and the Tyrone Guthrie Centre (Co.Monaghan) and it was during the first exchange of poets that I met James Simmons. We shared similar visions of how the education of a young poet might take place and when we finally got together in 1987 the talks began. I moved in with him in early autumn and we planned a move to an old coastguard station on the Antrim Coast, Northern Ireland. When The Poets' House had its first Summer Programme we ran three 10 day sessions. The first two sessions were attended by only a handful of students, but the word spread and frequently we had 20 or more. Seamus Heaney came the first year and the BBC recorded many of the readings. During this time I had my son Ben and lost another. Anna (my step-daughter) wrote her first Sestina at a summer session. She was 11 and using my poem *Every Solid Thing* as a guide; sitting in the back garden with her father, who was looking at my poem as well. He then wrote his *Sestina of The Sea Board*.

We were not breaking even, financially, but it didn't stop us—we had a vision and we were going to see it through.

I was very keen on setting up an MA in Creative Writing. I had my ideas about how I would like to see one taught. At this time Jimmy was the External

Examiner for Lancaster University, Lancashire, England. He approached Lancaster to see if they would validate the degree and to our delight, after negotiations, they agreed. So here were the tentative steps toward the first MA in Creative Writing in Ireland. In the first graduating cohort was Bridget Meeds (published in an introduction by Faber & Faber) and Terry Cafolla, successful screenwriter. Later Joe Woods, Paul Grattan, Mark Granier, Celia de Fréine, Matthew Donovan all came and graduated, and published or continued to publish. How lucky I have been! Hard work and luck is what a poet needs in order to hear the singing in his/her head that makes a poem. I have known very few wealthy poets, but many poets who are full of life.

Sherod Santos, Richard Tillinghast, and William Matthews offered advice and support in those early years. My first book *Settler* and Jimmy's *Mainstream* came out in 1995 with Salmon. The Poets' House moved to Falcarragh, Co. Donegal in late 1996; taking the three post-graduates to Donegal with us added to the adventure. The new Poets' House reflected my desire to have a beautiful space for poets to come together. We opened the doors in June, 1997. Jimmy was deeply happy in Donegal. The house was designed to be a teaching house. Our post graduate students in Donegal included Mary Reid, Matthew Fluharty, Adrian Fox, Joe Kane, Phil O'Connor, Annie Deppe and many others. Although Jimmy and I had never been happier, the constant financial drain of The Poets' House took its toll.

Jimmy's illness, and his subsequent death, deeply affected my life. But I picked up the pieces and struggled on until the last Falcarragh graduation in 2004. The success of the move from Falcarragh to Waterford was due to the hard work by me, John Ennis, and Greagoir O Duill who were both believers in The Poets' House. The Poets' House Centre Research Group at Waterford

Institute of Technology has recently graduated M.A.'s Rita Kelly, Marian Seyedi, Alan Garvey, Samantha Thomas and Garrett Fitzgerald, all publishing poems or fiction. In 1999 my *Starting At Purgatory* was published by Salmon, and in 2005 *The Bowsprit* (Lagan Press). My new book *St. Michael In Peril of The Sea* is due to be published by Salmon in May 2009.

Poets have to be willing to embrace life as it flows towards them. I still feel the magical space where meaning and sound, image and thought, are a living presence when I sit at journal or keyboard; when I open the door to workshop where students wait. And when term is over I drive north to my family home, to echoes of readings by Paul Durcan and Anthony Cronin, Medbh McGuckian and Eiléan Ní Chuilleanáin, to the echo of my husband's voice, to the pad of my old dog's ghost feet coming the length of the library. Falcarragh Poets' House. It is good to look back, but it is the next page that matters now.

Excerpt from memoir in progress

Recommended Reading:

The Changing Light at Sandover by James Merrill
The Comedia by Dante

Janice Fitzpatrick-Simmons has published three collections of poems. A fourth book is due to be published in spring of 2009. She has published in literary journals in Ireland, England and the USA and has appeared in anthologies including; *A Rage For Order, Poetry of The Troubles, The Backyards of Heaven, The Blackbird's Nest, Poets of Queen's University, Irish American Poets since 1800,* and *Salmon, A Journey in Poetry, 1981-2007.* She has read at literary festivals in Europe, the USA and in New Zealand. Janice (with her husband James Simmons) founded The Poets' House which offered the first creative writing MA in Ireland.

Kevin Higgins

(Galway, Ireland)

All Poetry's Children Under
The One Wide Roof

The reading series that I run, Over The Edge, provides a
platform for emerging writers, both poets and fiction
writers, who can read their work to a decent sized,
appreciative audience. It was born in Galway City Library
on Wednesday, January 22nd, 2003, when the first Over
The Edge: Open Reading took place. The featured
readers on that innocent Wednesday evening were poets
Maureen Gallagher and Caoilinn Hughes and fiction
writer Jim Mullarkey. The featured readers each read for
fifteen minutes. After they'd finished there was an open-
mic and members of the audience could read a poem or
short extract from a story or novel they were working on.
My good wife, Susan Millar DuMars, was the MC for the
evening. And that has remained the format ever since.

We guarantee new writers an audience for honing their
work. Our smallest crowd over the past six years has been
twenty five; our largest around ninety. The average of late
has been around fifty. It's not all the same crowd turning

up month after month. Different readers will draw different crowds. Our e-mail list, the key to the promotion of our readings, now runs to several thousand. At this stage, a decent percentage of the population of Galway City have attended at least one Over The Edge reading. One of the questions I always ask myself when we are lining up the featured readers for any given month is: what niche audience will each of them bring along? For example, are the members of a writers' group?

One of the featured readers at the sixth anniversary Over The Edge reading, on January 22nd, was Áine Tierney, a fiction writer who now lives back in her home county of Tipperary. Some years ago she did an MA in Writing at the National University of Ireland, Galway (NUIG) and used to work in our local post office in Newcastle. As I write this the post office is awash with posters for the reading and Áine's former workmates are all planning to come. One of the other readers is poet Tom French, who studied at NUIG and so is well known in these parts. My friend Gary King thinks my experience of tiny left wing meetings, during my long years as a member of the Militant Tendency, has filled me with a chronic fear of small crowds. He perhaps has a point. Since I turned forty I have less tolerance for many things, and none at all for the idea that it's impossible to get decent turnouts at poetry readings. If you have a positive attitude, an inclusive approach and most important of all, you persist, then your audience will grow.

That word 'inclusive' is much abused by politicians and poverty industry bureaucrats in search of votes and grants. What it means in this context is not that all poems or all poets are equal. To paraphrase George Orwell: some poems, some poets, are more equal than others. To deny that leads us towards the absurdity of pretending that, say, Shakespeare is no better nor worse a poet than those fledging male poets whose only outlet to date has been to scribble their masterpieces on the walls of public conveniences around Galway City. It's not that I haven't, from time to time, seen some snappy lines scrawled in such places. But, all things considered, Shakespeare is better. However, if one of Galway's toilet wall poets wants to come along and read at the open-mic, he would be very welcome. All must have an audience, if not necessarily a lasting reputation.

To properly understand the role Over The Edge plays it is necessary to see it in the context of the multiplicity of rigorous literary workshops which take place around Galway City, including the Galway Arts Centre, Galway Technical Institute, Galway Mayo Institute of Technology (GMIT) and the NUIG, MA in Writing. In any given month the majority of those who read at the open-mic are participants in one creative writing class or another. It is rarely a case of the wild unedited jottings of some Edgar Allan Poe in the making being given a histrionic airing (although that does occasionally happen) and far more often a case of poems in which a great deal of time, thought and consideration has been invested being given their first public hearing.

We use the open-mic as an unofficial audition for featured reader spots. Our job as events organisers and workshop facilitators (at last count Susan and I were facilitating twelve writing workshops a week between us) is not to make everyone a famous poet. Even if it were desirable, not everyone who puts words on paper is aiming for Faber and Faber or the Nobel Prize. For some, just getting their words down in the best way they can is what it's all about. They have other lives to attend to. That said many of those who began at the open-mic have gone on to be featured readers, to achieve publication and win major prizes.

In 2008 alone Mary Madec won the Hennessy Award for Poetry; Lorna Shaughnessy had her first collection,

Torching The Brown River, published by Salmon Poetry; and Miceál Kearney had his debut collection, *Inheritance*, published by Doire Press on foot of his victory in the North Beach Poetry Grand Slam. The next year or so will see the publication of first collections by six other Over The Edge alumni, Aideen Henry, John Corless, Elaine Feeney, John Walsh, Mary Madec and Celeste Augé, all by Salmon Poetry.

I first met Lorna Shaughnessy when she phoned me in October 2003 to say she had been writing poems "on the quiet" for a number of years and wanted someone to have a look at them. She was a featured reader at the December 2003 reading and also read at the first Cúirt/Over The Edge showcase reading in April 2006. A poem from Lorna's collection was included in this year's Forward Book of Poetry (The Forward Prize, London, England). Her days of doing it "on the quiet" are over.

When I first met Miceál Kearney he'd just started a Creative Writing for Beginners course at GMIT, facilitated by Susan, and was extremely nervous and monosyllabic. I was putting out chairs for the September 2005 Over The Edge: Open Reading and he asked me to put his name down for the open-mic. Since then he has won the Cúirt Festival, Galway, Poetry Grand Slam, The Baffle Festival prize and the Cúisle Festival Poetry Slam to name just a few; his work has appeared in journals such as The Shop, Orbis and Envoi; and he has read his work in Chicago, Brighton and Slovenia. These days, Miceál is a little less monosyllabic.

Perhaps the best example of what I'm talking about, though, was Mary Madec winning the 2008 Hennessy Award for Poetry. The Hennessy Award ceremony took place the week the Cúirt Festival was happening here. Mary had been selected to read at the now annual Cúirt/Over The Edge showcase reading. Each year we make a shortlist of those writers who've read for us and don't yet have a book published. The poets are then asked to submit three poems each which we pass on the Cúirt committee who choose the four or five writers to be showcased that particular year. It's a huge step forward for a bookless new writer to make it onto the programme of a festival such as Cúirt alongside the likes of Seamus Heaney, Nikki Giovanni & Edna O'Brien. And it's not at all tokenistic, but always rigorously competitive. We can never guess which of the short-listed writers will be chosen. Anyway, last year Mary Madec won the Hennessy and came back to Galway like the conquering heroine she was and performed brilliantly to a large audience on the main Cúirt stage at the Town Hall Theatre. RTE Radio's The Arts Show recorded the reading and interviewed Mary afterwards. I met Mary at a launch of *Crannóg* magazine in 2004. She was introduced to me as someone who "sometimes writes a few poems in her spare time." Since January 2005 Mary has been a valuable participant in the poetry workshops I facilitate at Galway Arts Centre. She sometimes writes poems while stuck in traffic jams. Nothing seems to stop her.

What makes Over The Edge work is the combination of openness and rigorous standards. If we think that you could hold your own reading for fifteen minutes alongside, say, Dennis O'Driscoll, Medbh McGuckian, Colette Bryce or Roddy Lumsden –to name just some of the established poets who've been featured readers at Over The Edge – then we will give you a chance. You might fly. Or you might fall a little flat. But either way, no-one will have died. One of our unpublished featured readers once spoke for seven minutes before reading a word of poetry. Most such early reading failures can be put down to nerves. And it is far better to be plagued with nerves than plagued with ego. Nerves you'll learn to control. And there would be something wrong if you weren't a little nervous the first time you're asked to do a fifteen minute reading with an established poet on the bill beside you! The first time I read my work in public at the Poets' Podium in Tralee, Co. Kerry, in March 1997, I was suitably terrified. But if you're a beginning poet, an overdose of ego will be the end of you. It will make you see constructive criticism as personal slight. Others will listen to the available advice, improve their poems and move on ahead of you. Then, of course, every success of theirs will hit you like a smack in the face. They'll win the Patrick Kavanagh Award, the Hennessy, the Nobel. They'll be published by Faber and invited to read in Athens and Tokyo. You'll either give up, or worse than that, you'll vanish down dark alleys and into whiskey bottles, consoling yourself with the fact that Kavanagh, too, was misunderstood in his day. I exaggerate... ever so slightly.

The final thing I'll say is that Over The Edge has no "political" agenda. We just want to make sure that every poet has his or her say and that, even if you disagree with what's being said, you listen. In October 2006, one of the featured readers was Yvonne Green, a widely published poet based in London, who describes herself as an "observant Jew and a Zionist". Yvonne closed her reading with a poem which was basically an attack on Hezbollah for, the poem implied, starting the 2006 war with Israel. She then said that she would be open to comments from the audience. I remember thinking "Hmmm. Now this could get interesting!" At that I looked at the clock and saw that it was 7.45pm. This meant that we had just fifteen minutes to complete the open mic. I am very much in favour of open mics being time-limited, but this was cutting it a bit fine. Since the library always closes at 8pm, I went out to tell the librarians that we might run a bit over time.

As I was on my way out Susan introduced the first

open-mic reader, a young school teacher from County Galway, who opened by saying that, following Yvonne's reference to the recent Israel-Hezbollah war he was now going to read a different poem from the one he'd originally intended. His poem took a pro-Palestinian view. I remember hearing the provocative line: "Did the Nazis teach you nothing?" as I exited the room and I was glad I was exiting. But everyone listened and no-one interrupted, just as they had listened to Yvonne. Just as they listened to Gordon Hewitt, the Derry-based performance poet and Socialist Workers Party member who got the audience, including my own mother, to participate in a sing song. At Over The Edge you'll find all poetry's children under the one wide roof. And that's as it should be.

Recommended Reading:

> *The Penguin Book of Socialist Verse* (Penguin, 1970),
>   Edited by Alan Bold
> *Philip Larkin Collected Poems* (Faber & Faber, 1988),
>   Edited with an introduction by Anthony Thwaite

Kevin Higgins was born in London in 1967, and grew up in Galway City where he still lives. He is co-organiser of the highly successful Over The Edge literary events. His two poetry collections are *The Boy With No Face* (Salmon, 2005) and, *Time Gentlemen, Please* (Salmon, 2008). *The Boy With No Face* was short-listed for the 2006 Strong Award and has recently gone to its second printing. One of the poems from *Time Gentlemen, Please*, 'My Militant Tendency', features in the *Forward Book of Poetry 2009*. He is the poetry critic of *The Galway Advertiser*. His work will be featured in the forthcoming anthology *Identity Parade – The New British and Irish Poets* (Bloodaxe, 2010). His third collection of poems *Frightening New Furniture* will be published by Salmon Poetry next year.

James Harrold

(Galway, Ireland)

The Poetry of Local Authorities

As you venture into the welcoming ranks of Kavanagh's standing army of Irish poets you will find a full adjutant corp of Local Authority Arts Officers ready, waiting and able to put our lives on the line for you in the service of poets and poetry in Ireland.

Every City and County Council in the Republic of Ireland now has a Local Authority Arts Office: Clare was established first, South Tipperary the last. Wherever you reside you are entitled to request the assistance of your Council in developing your talent. Like the Counties of Ireland we Arts Officers may vary a bit in personality and resources, but we are united in a common devotion to the needs of our artists and there is nothing we like better than to see a new local hero emerge triumphantly into print.

If you think you might have a vocation in poetry, but are unsure where to start, please talk to the staff in your local Arts Office. We can put you in touch with the local writing infrastructure. We help to establish new writing groups, and we advise on how best to manage them. We assist groups to organise readings, workshops and classes, bringing in established authors, linking up with national literary support organisations, facilitating you in weaving your work jointly and collectively into the vast and exciting tapestry of contemporary poetry in Ireland.

Many Arts Offices run writer-in-residence programmes where a dedicated writer develops an agreed programme for the local authority over a substantial period of time. Through workshops, masterclasses, evaluation, group and individual advice sessions the writer will come to know well the emerging authors and will assist them to find a voice and, perhaps, get published; often in a local authority anthology. There is now a substantial library of anthologies derived from residencies, featuring work of new and established writers.

I expect my writers-in-residence to have substantial experience of publishing in Ireland which they can put at the service of their flock. Good networkers at national and international level, their expertise, experience, good temper and literary savoir faire are squarely placed before their clients. Writer-in-residence programmes are generally co-funded by the Arts Council – the national body charged with developing the arts in Ireland. Over the years the Local Authorities and the Arts Council have established a close rapport strongly manifested in our programme of joint residencies, many of which have become models of best practise.

Arts Officers can help you to make arts centres and literary festivals work for you and we are happy to put you into the great Irish cultural mix, learning from the work of invited writers or participating yourself at whatever level suits you, from making your debut in a Saturday morning group to reading your latest prizewinning Faber or Salmon collection to a rapt sell-out audience in Strokestown, Listowel, Galway or Dun Laoghaire,

Depending on resources, Arts Offices can supply bursaries towards developing your individual artistic practise. Contact your local Arts Office for details, as requirements and application rules may vary. The Arts Office staff will be extremely helpful in taking you through the process. Awards to individuals are generally cash grants but could also take other forms such as residencies at the wonderful Tyrone Guthrie Centre, travel bursaries, international networking and the manifold innovative means to a creative end that might occur to a proactive and resourceful Arts Officer.

Local Authorities also fund (and in many cases administer) the theatres, libraries, arts centres and festivals where poetry is showcased. If you become a literary impresario, you will need to stay in touch with your local Arts Office.

And (apart from that bit in the second paragraph) there is nothing an Arts Officer likes better than a writer dropping in for a chat or a brainstorm, for together we can plan adventures. A wizened old Arts Officer now I find my mind wandering from the latest dreary Community and Enterprise memo and back to the memories: to Pat Boran emerging on a snowy Connemara night to enthral and empower Letterfrack Writers Group: to sparkling Michael O'Loughlin exchanging gossip, politics and poetics with senior citizens in Ballybane Library; Pat O'Brien designing a festival deep in rural Skehanagh whilst Tom Kenny and Vinnie Browne sniff the air for Cúirt; I see again heroic Mary O'Malley en route to a workshop coping with a winter puncture in the dark and rainy Inagh Valley, Michael D. Higgins cross-legged on the floor of the Arts Office van, rattling joyfully across East Galway, a capacity Portumna audience in prospect; Desmond O'Grady declaiming on Greek myth to a hushed and happy house in Canavans bar, the Tuam writers devotedly (and literally) sitting at his feet; Seamus Heaney exchanging poems with schoolchildren on a sunny Salthill Promenade; Johnny Choll Mhaidhc, eyes closed, reciting at the Kinvara Cruinniu out of his powerful memory his true poet's response to Raftery; or a community hall audience overflowing out onto the ancient battlefield, Richard Murphy leading a confabulation of poets and musicians revisiting on the night of its 300th anniversary his great verse meditation of the battle of Aughrim. Then I am disturbed from my reverie by a call from Michael about a new series of masterclasses he means to hold in the City Museum and tonight *Over the Edge* is on in the City Library...

All Arts Officers can reveal similar memories. We are privileged to work with Ireland's artists and audiences and we are always at your service, looking for the next poet to work with. Just call in to your local Council office and let the adventure begin!

James Harrold is Galway City Arts Officer. Formerly, he was Artistic Director of Wexford Arts Centre and Galway County Arts Officer. He has also worked with Cúirt International Literature Fetsival, Galway Arts Centre, Galway Arts Festival and Macnas.

Selected Web Resources

IRELAND

Salmon Poetry
www.salmonpoetry.com

Poetry Ireland
www.poetryireland.ie/resources/getting-published

The Dublin Writers' Workshop
www.dublinwriters.org

The Irish Writers' Centre
www.writerscentre.ie

DLR Poetry Now International Poetry Festival
www.poetrynow.ie

The Munster Literature Centre
www.munsterlit.ie

Over the Edge, Galway
www.overtheedgeliteraryevents.blogspot.com

The Western Writers' Centre, Galway
www.twwc.ie

The Stinging Fly
www.stingingfly.org

Creative writing workshops on the Costa de la Luz, Spain
www.inthewritelight.com

The Whitehouse Poetry Readings, Limerick
www.gleesonwhitehouse.com/poetry_corner.htm

Dead Drunk Dublin, online literary arts magazine
www.deaddrunkdublin.com

Virtual Writer – Creative Writing, Literary New & Reviews (Longford)
www.virtualwriter.net

SoundEye – Irish Poetry & Writing
www.soundeye.org

The Arts Council of Ireland
www.artscouncil.ie

UNITED KINGDOM

The Poetry Kit
www.poetrykit.org

The Poetry Society
www.poetrysociety.org.uk

The Poetry Library, Southbank Centre
www.poetrylibrary.org.uk

The Poetry Archive
www.poetryarchive.org

Poetry Scotland
www.poetryscotland.co.uk

Poetry in Wales
www.walesindex.co.uk/pages/307.html

Poetry Magazines Archive – The Poetry Library, Southbank Centre
www.poetrymagazines.org.uk

Atlas: New Writing, Art & Image | Aark Arts
www.atlasaarkarts.zoomshare.com

dumbfoundry
www.dumbfoundry.blogspot.com

Kudos | Orbis Literary International Journal
www.kudoswriting.wordpress.com

The Poem
www.thepoem.co.uk/about.htm

Poetry London
www.poetrylondon.co.uk

nthposition
www.nthposition.com/poetry.

Oxfam Marylebone Bookshop
www.oxfammarylebone.co.uk

PoetCasting – Poetry podcasting project
www.poetcasting.co.uk

Poetry PF
www.poetrypf.co.uk

Shadowtrain Magazine
www.shadowtrain.com

The Argotist Online
www.argotistonline.co.uk

USA

Poets and Writers' Journal
www.pw.org

The Poetry Market
www.thepoetrymarket.com

About.com – Poetry
www.poetry.about.com

Poetry Daily
www.poems.com

The Poetry Resource Page
www.poetryresourcepage.com

Writers Write – Poetry section
www.writerswrite.com/poetry

The Poetry Society of America
www.poetrysociety.org

Contrary Magazine
www.contrarymagazine.com

Hanger's Poetry Resources
www.hangtide.com/poetryresources

Library of Congress Poetry Resources
www.loc.gov/rr/program/bib/lcpoetry

StumbleUpon – Poetry
www.stumbleupon.com/tag/poetry/

Poetry Express
www.poetryexpress.org

Poetry Magazine
www.poetrymagazine.com

Poets Online
www.poetsonline.org

Poets and Writers Blog
http://poetsandwriters.com/

Wikipedia – Poetry
en.wikipedia.org/wiki/Poetry

Open Directory Project – Poetry
www.dmoz.com/Arts/Writers_Resources/Poetry/

Google – Magazines & Ezines
http://directory.google.com/Top/Arts/Literature/Poetry/Mag
azines_and_E-zines/

Poetry Super Highway
www.poetrysuperhighway.com

Poets.org – The Academy of American Poets
www.poets.org

Terrain.org
www.terrain.org

Writers' Digest
www.writersdigest.com

The Poetry Foundation – publisher of Poetry Magazine
www.poetryfoundation.org

Shadow Poetry
www.shadowpoetry.com

E-Ratio Modern Poetry
www.eratiopostmodernpoetry.com

CANADA

Northern Poetry Review
www.northernpoetryreview.com

Poetry Canada Magazine
www.poetrycanada.com

The League of Canadian Poets
www.poets.ca

Canadian Poetry Association
www.canadianpoetryassoc.com

AUSTRALIA

PressPress
www.presspress.com.au

Jacket Magazine
www.jacketmagazine.com

Australian Poetry Centre
www.australianpoetrycentre.org.au

Australian Bush Verse, Poetry & Music
www.bushverse.com

Cordite Poetry Review
www.cordite.org.au

NEW ZEALAND

New Zealand Poets
www.poetry.org.nz

New Zealand Electronic Poetry Centre
www.nzepc.auckland.ac.nz